Sault Ste. Marie and Beyond
A History of Its People
17th – 21st Centuries

Including Upper Peninsula MI and
Mackinac Island 1600s – 1700s

Sandra Rousseau

Published by Awaken Ink Inc. 2018
Sault Ste. Marie, Ontario

ISBN
978-1-989142-17-2

Inside Front Cover: Old Woman Bay, Lake Superior
by Sheri Minardi Photography

Map of the Great Lakes areas, located in the
Ermatinger-Clergue National Historic Site, Sault Ste.
Marie, ON
Photo taken by Corey Marques, Publisher

Table of Contents

Introduction

The Anishinaabe have been firmly established in the Sault for thousands of years. The French thought they discovered the upper Great Lakes about four hundred years ago but it was the other way around. The Indigenous discovered the French when they came paddling up the river, right up to the Ojibway homes. About two hundred years later, European immigrants believed that they 'settled' the area but, again, the area had been 'settled' long ago.

Luke Dalla Bona, a highly accomplished archaeologist, discovered artifacts of people who lived "from about 10,000 years ago until the present" in the Gros Cap area.

Formerly of the Sault, Dalla Bona conducted archaeological assessments of the Gros Cap Bluffs and later Chene Island. These two areas are just west of the Sault, at the southeast corner of Lake Superior, near the entrance into the St. Marys River.

Separately, there are ongoing DNA studies of ancient skeletal remains of Indigenous people to determine their origin. Of interest to us is that haplogroup X2a, which is the rarest of the North American mitochondrial DNA haplogroups, was centered in and around Sault Ste. Marie.

The studies of Deborah Bolnick, Ph.D., indicate that mtDNA haplogroup X2a has not been seen in Europe or in Asia. She suggests that X2a could be up to 40,000 years old, originating in the Holy Land, and the Hills of Galilee in particular.

Two artifacts were found in the U.S. that, presumably, tie our Indigenous people to the ancient Hebrew language. Looking at the religious beliefs of Indigenous ancestors shows that parallels exist with the Hebrews, for example, the Ten Commandments. Some have declared the artifacts as being hoaxes, but more recently, studies are suggesting that they are legitimate.

I hope it is not getting too late to dig up more extremely ancient artifacts.

Whitefish Island is situated in the St. Marys River, beside the Canadian canal. Parks Canada states that Indigenous people continually occupied this island since it was geologically created more than 2,000 years ago. Until the early 1900s, the Ojibway resided here. Although still reserved for the Ojibway, it is now a park setting with a National Historic Site designation where there is considerable wild life. One day, while out walking, I saw a young fox running along the road near the Locks and was told that there is a den of foxes on White Fish Island.

Originally, Sault Ste. Marie was one settlement, incorporating both banks of its turbulent rapids until a line was drawn, by the powers that were, along the length of the St. Marys River which split the settlement between two countries. "St. Marys" is not grammatically correct, but that is just how it came to be.

The Ojibway, being Canadian, and the Chippewa, of the United States, who are the same people, gave the name Baawitigong, to the area surrounding the rapids. This spelling evolved to Bawating, which some say means fast rushing waters. Others claim that it means place of the rapids or meeting place. Each translation is fitting. It was a meeting place for Indigenous people who travelled here from a distance of a few hundred miles between spring and fall each year. From a very small population, perhaps 100 to 200 people, Bawating expanded to accommodate about 2,000 Indigenous people during their annual social and fishing season.

Ojibway is a main section of the Anishinaabe Indigenous people. Anishinaabe means *original people* which is a very appropriate description of them. The Anishinaabe incorporate various Indigenous groups in both Canada and the U.S., including Ojibway, Chippewa, Potawatomi, Odawa/Ottawa, Oji-Cree, Mississauga, and Algonquin. All are culturally related.

I will now refer to Parks Canada Manuscript Report Number 439, which dates back to 1979. This was an extensive report which I will not detail here, except to quote from it at page 55: The authors of the report made an interesting comment regarding the Ojibway evolution post-European intervention in their lives:

> His language and social customs still survived with considerable strength. In fact, the Ojibwa, whose lifestyle was based on an acceptance of his environment not its transformation, survived the impact of the Euro-Canadian civilization, diseases and wars better than any other group in the Upper Great Lakes.

* * *

As clerks in the fur trade, four of my ancestors married Indigenous women. All of them spent much time on St. Joseph Island, Mackinac Island, Drummond Island, the Sault, and Michipicoten. This is why I came to be intrigued by this area.

Bets were placed and off they went amid much cheering.

Canoe Race Near Sault Ste. Marie 1836
by George Catlin

Seventeenth Century

Étienne Brûlé, the First Explorer

As we all know from our elementary school days, and which the local plaque at the locks reminds us, the first European explorer to visit our area was a French fellow named Étienne Brûlé. His actual surname was Bruslé but he became known as Brûlé.

It cannot be confirmed that Brûlé was with Samuel de Champlain during Champlain's first fight with the Iroquois in the summer of 1610; however, it was the following day when Brûlé asked Champlain if he could go off to live with the Huron Indigenous people.

Champlain was all in favour of this because he wanted interpreters. He also expected Brûlé to help with colonization although it is not clear whether Champlain explained this to him. Brûlé was quite young, at age eighteen, when he went with the Algonquin War Chief, Iroquet, to live with his tribe in what is now Ontario. There was an interesting deal struck in that Brûlé went to the Iroquet tribe, also known as the Huron nation, and a young Huron, who Champlain called Savignon, went with Champlain.

C.W. Butterfield in *Brûlé's Discoveries and Explorations* explained that the exchange was an idea put forward by Iroquet to provide security for both youths.

One year later, about June 13, 1611, Brûlé returned to Champlain, dressed like his Huron friends, fluently speaking their language, and obviously accepted by them as one of their own. It was apparent that he had gained considerable cultural as well as geographical knowledge.

The Huron fellow had not changed during his time away from his tribe, even though he had travelled to France with Champlain. It is not known how long the Indigenous fellow was in France, but it would have been my guess that, considering the major differences in culture, there would have been an impact on the young Huron, at least in some ways, but apparently this was not the case.

At the conclusion of their reunion, Champlain was satisfied with the progress that Brûlé had made over the past year, and he then expected that Brûlé would begin to work toward building a cultural bridge between the colonists and the Indigenous people.

Without so much as a 'goodbye, I'll see you soon,' Brûlé disappeared.

It is believed that he went to live with the Hurons at Toanché in Penetanguishene Bay, in southeast Georgian Bay, near present day Midland, Ontario. He may have been the first European to travel the Ottawa-Mattawa-Lake Nipissing-French River-Georgian Bay route.

Further contact was made with Champlain at some point; otherwise Brûlé's story would have ended here.

According to Champlain's journals and *Jesuit Relations*, Butterfield pieced together Brûlé's travels, as much as could be determined. He believed that Brûlé and his friend, Grenolle, reached Lake Superior between 1621 and 1623. There was confusion regarding Brûlé's activities because he was a case of 'now you see him – now you don't.' Many gaps could not be filled in.

Gabriel Sagard, a lay brother of the Recollet Order, who was the historian of the Recollets' travels, wrote that Brûlé had shown him a piece of copper. Grenolle gave a description of the Indigenous person who had provided the copper. That description was of the Anishinaabe who lived on the North Channel of Lake Huron.

Grenolle did not give the description directly to Sagard, but to a third party. Through reasoning, it was decided that the copper had been acquired from an Anishinaabe living on the North Channel of Lake Huron.

From the North Channel, they probably continued west via the St. Marys River until they entered Lake Superior. The difficulty is that Sagard was not explicit in his writing but only implied that Brûlé had been to Lake Superior. Sagard further wrote:

> The Interpreter Bruslé and a
> number of Indians have assured
> us that beyond the mer douce
> [Lake Huron] there is another
> very large lake, which empties

into the former by a waterfall,
nearly two leagues across,
which has been called the
Gaston falls.

Is this statement meant to prove that Brûlé
had been in that area, or was he repeating
statements made to him by Indigenous people?
Apart from that, "nearly two leagues across" is the
equivalent of nearly six miles [10 km]. Father
Claude Allöuez wrote, in 1665, that the rapids were
"half a league," being 1.5 miles [2.5 km] across.

Another question comes to mind. Who named
Gaston falls? It is not an Indigenous name. Sagard
also stated "a number of Indians" confirmed the
description of the area as well as the name Gaston.
Apart from the geographical description, does
Sagard's statement imply that the rapids at the
Sault were already named Gaston, before Brûlé's
time? It appears that it is not definitely known if
Brûlé named the rapids, or if it was another
unreported Frenchman who had given the rapids
the name of Sault du Gaston, presumably in
honour of the brother of the King of France.

Grace Lee Nute, in her book entitled *Lake
Superior*, states that *Jesuit Relations* does not, for
the first time, refer to Lake Superior until 1647 –
1648. Nute further explains that:

By 1623 missionaries among the Huron Indians
had learned from these two men [Brûlé and
Grenolle] and possibly others that there was
"another very great lake" above Lake Huron,
into which it poured by **rapids already bearing
the name of the king's brother, the Sault de
Gaston** [emphasis added].

Otto Fowle, in his book entitled *Sault Ste. Marie and Its Great Waterway*, stated "Father Sagard, in his writing, first tried to fix upon the village by the falls the name Sault de Gaston, in honour of a prominent Frenchman."

Champlain, on the other hand, always referred to the area as "the Sault" in his journal.

In any event, Brûlé has been credited with giving that name to our area.

It is believed that Brûlé gave the geographical information to Champlain, who then created a map, in 1632, showing the Grand Lac [later Lake Superior] and the river joining it to Lake Huron, with Indigenous settlements depicted on both sides of the river. At this time, the river remained unnamed, only receiving its name nine years later.

Champlain had a problem with Brûlé because he knew that he was working for certain businessmen in Québec rather than for colonization. It is true that the merchants were paying Brûlé a yearly salary for persuading the Indigenous people to trade with them. As to closing the cultural gap between the French and the Indigenous people, I am not sure what Brûlé could have done.

Apart from this, in 1629, Brûlé jumped canoe, so to speak, by joining the employ of England's Kirke brothers once they had captured Québec from Champlain.

That did it! There ensued an altercation between Champlain and Brûlé wherein Champlain accused Brûlé of being a traitor. Brûlé, being outraged, took off again, for the last time.

Champlain wrote that Brûlé was "very vicious in character, and much addicted to women." Addicted to woman? No details of the alleged addiction were disclosed, but this may have been why Brûlé was murdered by the Hurons in 1633 at age 41. No one knows exactly who killed him, or why, but the Hurons afterward regretted his death to the extent that they left their village and set up a new village in a nearby location.

It appears that Brûlé's death had nothing to do with survival in the wilderness but everything to do with the wild side of his personality.

Champlain told that Brûlé was the first and only Frenchman, at least at that time, to shoot the Sault-Saint-Louis [Lachine] rapids in a canoe and that he, Champlain, had not done it on his own but with the help of some Indigenous people.

Unfortunately for us, Brûlé did not keep a journal of his activities or a chart of his travels. Given Champlain only referred to Brûlé once by name, historians have gone to much effort to try to piece together Brûlé's travels.

There is no documentation suggesting that any other French explorers were in the Sault after Brûlé's visit, until Jean Nicolet arrived.

Soon after his arrival in Québec, in 1618, Nicolet arranged to live with the Algonquins on Allumettes Island, on the Ottawa River, north of Pembroke, Ontario.

According to *Jesuit Relations*, within his first two years of travelling with the Algonquins, he often went a week without food, and on one journey, he ate bark from the trees for seven weeks. For many years, Nicolet passed for one of the Algonquins, taking part in their councils, while fishing and trading for himself.

Nicolet arrived at, or near, the Sault, in August of 1634, having been sent by Champlain to find the Northwest Passage to Asia. He made his way by birch bark canoe, along with seven men of the Huron Nation, via the Ottawa-Mattawa-Lake Nipissing-French River-Georgian Bay route which was the quickest and safest way to travel from Québec to our area. It was safest because the route did not cross Iroquois territory. At that time, the Iroquois did not get along with anyone at all!

There is no record that Nicolet communicated with the Anishinaabe at the Sault, so I can only assume that he must not have stayed long, or perhaps not at all, before he continued on to Lake Michigan. Many descriptions of Nicolet's travels state that he went from Lake Huron to the straits of Mackinac, and then into Lake Michigan.

Just before presumably reaching China, he removed his French clothing and put on a multi-colour damask robe, intending to stage a grand entrance into the Orient. I cannot imagine what he said when he discovered that he had arrived at, what is now, Green Bay, Wisconsin.

Nicolet's goal, in addition to finding the Northwest Passage, was to get to know the Indigenous people living beyond Lake Huron, with a view to extending the French fur trade. How successful he was with this is not known, but he was credited with helping the Jesuit priests, during his travels, in their attempts to teach Christianity to the Indigenous people.

After spending the winter with the Winnebago Tribe, as the first Frenchman to visit the area, Nicolet made his way back to Québec, arriving there in 1635.

He survived the wilderness, but died prematurely on October 29, 1642, in a shipwreck near Sillery, Québec, leaving a young wife, a daughter and a son.

The Priests

At Champlain's request, four priests of the Recollet fraternity, which was one of the Franciscan orders, arrived in Québec in 1615, to establish missions and teach Christianity to the Indigenous people.

The highly educated priests were required to keep accurate records of their work and travels so that, in addition to their Christian teachings, they became historians and geographers. Without their records, we would not know our seventeenth century history.

The transition from France to Canada must have been quite a jolt to them because they had left the most advanced civilization in the world to come to live among the uncivilized.

Between 1634 and 1649 the missions did rather well, although they never had much luck converting anyone to Christianity. The Jesuits' goal was to create a nation of Indigenous Christians, without interference by non-Indigenous people, but governed by the Roman Catholic Church.

Often, Indigenous people arrived at the missions to trade, for social interaction, or due to fear of Iroquois attacks. Except for the Iroquois, other Indigenous nations were respectful of the priests, and although they did not understand why the priests wanted them to become Catholics, the Indigenous were in awe of the pomp and ceremony conducted by the priests. The end result was that the priests concentrated on teaching the Indigenous children, hoping that those children would then teach Christianity to their parents. The adults were unwilling to commit to Catholicism but whatever their feelings were; they did not demonstrate any opposition to the priests' teachings.

Given that the Indigenous were always on the move for purposes of hunting and fishing, the priests did not have their attention long enough to instruct them. If the priests had stayed in missions along the St. Lawrence River, they would normally only have the summers to interact with the Indigenous. To do the best they could, they went along with the Indigenous on their journeys in search of food.

The priests' normal clothing style was not at all conducive to tramping through the rugged terrain of forests, swamps, rivers, ice and snow. Their feet were bare; they wore wood sandals along with a hooded gown made out of coarse material. They were often extremely cold but persevere they did.

In April, 1632, Father Paul Le Jeune, of the Society of Jesus, sailed from France to Québec, and wrote about his journey to Rev. Father Barthelemy Jacquinot which letter is contained in *Jesuit Relations Vol. V*. He told that there was good sailing weather at the beginning which allowed them to cover about 600 leagues (1,800 miles) in ten days; however, over the next 30 days, barely 200 leagues were travelled. During May and some of June, there was such a cold wind that the priests suffered from frozen limbs. The food was deplorable because everything was salted which caused continual thirst, and there was not a drop of fresh water to drink. Their cabins were so small that they could not stand upright, kneel down, or even be seated, and when it rained, the water hit Le Jeune's face.

On Pentecost day, he was about to preach, when one of the sailors called out, "Codfish! Codfish!" With that pronouncement, the sermon was forgot, and everyone focused on cod fishing. Father Le Jeune wrote that the fish were "very welcome to us after such continuous storms."

In late May, he saw two huge icebergs that were longer than their ship and higher than their masts. Fortunately, there was no collision.

On June 1, they spotted land, covered in snow, and on June 3, passed into the St. Lawrence River, arriving at Québec City on July 5, 1632, two months and 18 days after leaving France.

Regarding the Indigenous people, Father Le Jeune described how cruel they were in their torture of their enemies: killing them, half-burning them, and then eating their flesh. He further wrote:

> Let no one be astonished at these acts of barbarism. Before the faith was received in Germany, Spain, or England, those nations were not more civilized. Mind is not lacking among the Savages of Canada, but education and instruction.

The Indigenous

As we know, the Indigenous people moved for purposes of hunting and fishing, and because of this the territories of the various Indigenous nations overlapped. All were multilingual and similar in looks and habits. As well, part of their culture involved marrying outside of their own tribe. As a result, it was impossible for the priests to classify them, although I am not sure why they would need to.

The Iroquois had distinct branches that waged war against each other and terrorized all the other Indigenous nations. The main Iroquois tribes lived south and east of Lakes Erie and Ontario. This allowed them to control the waterways adjoining these lakes. It is estimated that there were about 17,000 of them, a small number considering the havoc they caused for other Indigenous, as well as everyone else in Canada and the U.S.A.

The Hurons were related to the Iroquois but for some unknown reason were normally at war with them.

Champlain made friends with the Hurons and Algonquins, who were his neighbours, and fought with them against the Iroquois which was a huge mistake on his part. I suppose it was natural for him to do this. As a result, there was a permanent atmosphere of hostility between the French and the Iroquois.

Champlain was so busy defending the French from the Iroquois in Québec that he had no time to leave the area to explore elsewhere.

His preoccupation with the Iroquois made Champlain vulnerable to be overtaken by the English, which is what happened between the years 1629 and 1632.

The Jesuits tried to persuade the Indigenous to put down roots and take up agriculture to give the priests a better chance to teach Christianity to them.

In the early days of the missions, the Jesuits brought the French and Indigenous together.

On a commercial level, it would have been a poor business decision for the Indigenous to stay in one place, as this would have been too great a hindrance to trapping furs.

The fur trade was important to the Indigenous because it was the only way that they could acquire the European goods they wanted.

Later, the Jesuits opposed the fur traders in their practice of giving rum to the Indigenous. A useful tactic by French fur traders, to gain their friendship and trade, was to supply rum to the Indigenous, who immediately became addicted to it.

Eventually, the fur traders, who were only concerned with making money for themselves, began to oppose the Jesuits.

What developed was an Indigenous tug-of-war between the priests and the fur traders.

To the Sault by Invitation

According to *Jesuit Relations*, the year 1641 brought Fathers Isaac Joques and Charles Raymbault to the Sault from their home with the Hurons at Ste. Marie, on the northeast corner of Wye Lake which is near Midland, Ontario. Wye Lake joins Wye River which in turn meets southeastern Georgian Bay.

The Indigenous from the Sault had been at Ste. Marie to take part in a Feast for the Dead, being a ceremony attended by a few thousand Indigenous participants from a radius of several hundred miles.

Dr. Milo M. Quaife, a professional American historian, described the festivities:

"several days dances, feasts, and athletic contests were held. There was even a greased-pole-climbing contest, which one resourceful savage won by a clever trick."

It is too bad that Quaife did not let us in on the clever trick.

The priests did everything they could, including giving presents and preparing feasts, to win over the Indigenous people. They presented themselves so well that the Indigenous people from the Sault asked the Jesuit priests to come to visit them.

Father Charles Raymbault, who had spent considerable time with the Algonquins in the Nipissing area, was able to communicate with the Anishinaabe from the Sault because they shared the same language, so it was that he came to travel to the Sault for a visit.

Some Hurons, as well as Father Jogues, who spoke the language of the Hurons, went along for the ride.

According to *Jesuit Relations*, after travelling by canoe for seventeen days, the priests reached Bawating, about October 4, 1641, where they found approximately 2,000 Indigenous.

The Anishinaabe asked the priests to remain and reside at Bawating. To this invitation, the priests readily agreed on the understanding that the Indigenous would be amenable to learning the Christian religion. Of course, the Indigenous had no clue about Christianity but being impressed with the priests, they agreed.

When the Priests learned that there were more Indigenous to the west of the Sault, they realized that there were many more people to convert to Christianity. However, according to Quaife, the priests returned to their home in Huronia because they did not have enough priests to cover both Huronia and Bawating.

Otto Fowle in his book, *Sault Ste. Marie and Its Great Waterway*, explained that a permanent mission was not established because the Iroquois were attacking the Saulteurs to exterminate them. This would give the Iroquois the fur trade all to themselves.

Jesuit Relations credited Fathers Joques and Raymbault with establishing a mission at the Sault, but there was no mention of an actual building or hut having been constructed; however, according to Quaife, these priests were credited with naming the river after their patron, Sainte Marie (Saint Mary).

Father Raymbault at age forty, although robust, became seriously ill and was taken back to Québec in the spring of 1642. In the fall of that year, he became the first Jesuit to die in Québec. Given he was held in such high esteem, the Governor arranged to have him buried beside Champlain.

Father Joques was taken prisoner by the Iroquois and was put through terrible torture, the nasty details of which I will leave out. Fortunately, he escaped death when rescued by the Dutch of Albany and was sent back to France. He did return to Québec in 1644 but in October 1646, at the age of thirty-seven years, was killed by a Mohawk.

The Saulteurs

Incidentally, by 1648, *Jesuit Relations* was referring to the lake above the St. Marys River as Lake Superior because it was higher and larger than lakes Michigan and Huron.

The Saulteurs (so-teur) or Saulteaux (so-toe) were so named by the French because they lived on each side of the rapids; however, among themselves, they are known as Anishinaabe or Anishinaabek. It is thought that they numbered about 25,000 persons in the seventeenth century.

The Sault (Bawating) was one of their dwelling places, but not the only one, because they travelled in accordance with the seasons for hunting and fishing. The tribe was spread over a wide area around Lake Superior, but Bawating was where they came together for social meetings while fishing in the summer and fall of each year for whitefish.

They fought with the Sioux and the Foxes to the west at the same time that they were being attacked by the Iroquois from the east. With this in mind, their fighting skills must have been well honed. Fighting with the Sioux was carried on over about two hundred years with the result that the Sioux moved west to the plains. At some point, the Foxes were pushed out of the area towards the middle of Wisconsin.

It appears that the Iroquois wanted to do business with the Dutch in the fur trade, and therefore, wanted to do away with any opposition, being the French and other Indigenous people, especially those of the upper Great Lakes who had been travelling to Québec by way of the Ottawa River, with beaver skins. The Iroquois were given guns by the Dutch of New York state which put them at an advantage in warfare.

During the Iroquois wars, many tribes had migrated to upper Michigan and Wisconsin to get away from the dreaded Iroquois.

Meanwhile, the Iroquois were all over the place which included hiding along the Ottawa River to ambush the Indigenous people travelling to Québec with their furs.

People in Québec were suffering commercially due to lack of furs to sell to Europe, as well as suffering physically from constant Iroquois attacks on their homes and inhabitants.

By 1652, the Algonquins banded together, with about a thousand warriors from several tribes, in an area about three days' travelling west of the Sault, in anticipation of an Iroquois attack.

Several hundred Iroquois travelled to this area, in 1653, to wage war. Their problem became finding wild game along the way. Due to their weakened physical state, they made peace, following which they headed south. Very soon, they realized they had been duped. The Algonquins had given them poisoned corn bread.

The Iroquois again decided to fight, but this time further away. One group headed south where it was beaten by the Illinois, while the other group went north.

Once this group arrived at Iroquois Point, in Whitefish Bay, on the south side of Lake Superior, near the Sault, the Saulteurs attacked them with arrows and clubs. The Iroquois had guns but that did not matter. They were soundly defeated.

The Iroquois then promptly approached the French in Lower Canada (Quebec) to enter into a peace agreement.

After several years of hunting for furs but not being able to travel to Québec, due to Iroquois attacks, a lengthy fleet of canoes arrived in Quebec from the upper Great Lakes, in 1654, carrying furs that turned Quebec's economy completely around.

It can be said that our Ojibway Saulteurs saved the day for our fledgling country. Unbeknown to them, they rescued Québec from total financial ruin and created a safe environment for all people.

When the Indigenous returned to their homelands, Groseilliers and another Frenchman travelled with them. It had been reported that the other Frenchman was Radisson; however, there is documented proof that Radisson was in Québec, signing a Deed on November 7, 1655.

The following year, overloaded with valuable furs, Groseilliers made a return trip to Québec.

After this first trip to the west, Groseilliers told the Jesuit priests in Québec about the Indigenous people in what is now northern Wisconsin.

As a result of this communication, and after some delays, Father René Ménard arrived in the west, four years later.

Ojibway Sault Ste. Marie 1846
by Paul Kane (1810 – 1871). Wiki2

Médard Chouart, Sieur des Groseilliers, and Pierre-Esprit, Sieur de Radisson, who were brothers-in-law, left Trois-Rivières in Québec, in August of 1659. On their voyage to the Sault, they had the companionship of a group of Saulteurs.

There were many days when they went without any food at all. The Saulteurs kept telling them not to worry because as soon as they got to the Sault, there would be hundreds of whitefish to eat. They would be the finest fish they had ever tasted. The fish would each weigh twelve pounds. No chance of starving at the Sault. Radisson and Groseilliers had trouble believing their friends.

Upon arrival at the Sault, they found that the Anishinaabe had not been kidding them as an all-you-can-eat fish fry was quickly prepared. Radisson wrote that they also feasted on bear, beaver, and moose while at the Sault. It is not known how long they stayed but it was long enough that Radisson reported that they made cottages for themselves.

Toward the end of autumn, they paddled on to spend the winter with Huron and Ottawa Indigenous people, who had taken refuge from the Iroquois, likely at Lac Courte-Oreille (Lake Short Ear), or Ottawa Lake, in Wisconsin.

Radisson wrote that it was a hard winter with more than enough snow, but the worst part was watching so many Indigenous die of starvation. The Frenchmen were not faring well either. Groseilliers' face was so emaciated from lack of nourishment that it could barely be seen beneath his heavy beard.

The Indigenous invited Radisson and Groseilliers to participate in their Feast of the Dead, held at some point during the winter, to which many other nations came. There are no details regarding the feast, but perhaps it was potluck, considering the lack of available food in the area that winter. It is assumed that the visiting Indigenous provided Radisson and Groseilliers with information regarding lands to the west, and to Hudson Bay, and as to the vast extent of beavers in those areas, given there was no time for Radisson and Groseilliers to have travelled to Hudson Bay.

Following the feast, Radisson and Groseilliers travelled into the Sioux territory where they stayed for six weeks, after which, during the spring, they returned to Lake Superior, crossing its north side, while visiting the Cree in that area. It is possible that they may have picked up more information from the Cree about fur trading possibilities further to the north.

About August 20, 1660, in the company of approximately three hundred Indigenous, they arrived back at Trois-Rivières, Quebec, loaded with furs valued at 200,000 livres that were sufficient in worth to ensure that the French colony would not have to file for bankruptcy.

I cannot understand why the Governor was so upset with them, but he was. Instead of celebrating the accomplishments of Radisson and Groseilliers, the governor instructed his officials to confiscate most of their furs and, if that was not insulting enough, the two men were heavily fined for not obtaining the Governor's permission before engaging in the fur trade.

I imagine that the Indigenous people were expecting to acquire goods that were important to them when the furs were handed over; however, there is no documentation as to how they fared on this unfortunate transaction.

Radisson and Groseilliers appealed to the authorities in France but did not receive the backing that was due them.

As a result of this unfair treatment, they made arrangements, during the following several years, to provide their geographical knowledge, as well as the status of beavers in that area, to the English.

With this knowledge, the English, along with Radisson and Groseilliers, formed the Hudson's Bay Company in 1670, with the blessing of England's King Charles II, which would prove to be a nasty blow to the French!

Radisson and Groseilliers
　　　Painting by Archibald Bruce Stapleton

Voyageur Canoe
Painting by Frances Anne Hopkins (1838 – 1919)

Scene showing a large Hudson's Bay Company
freight canoe passing a waterfall, presumably on
the French River. The passengers in the canoe may
be the artist, Frances Anne Hopkins, and her
husband, Edward Hopkins, secretary to the
Governor of the Hudson's Bay Company.

This image is available from Library and Archives
Canada under the reproduction reference number
C-002771 and under the MIKAN ID number
Licensed under Public Domain via Commons
https://wiki2.org/en/File:Voyageur_canoe.jpg#/me
dia/File:Voyageur_canoe.jpg

Father René Ménard

It was 1660, and Father René Ménard, at age 55
years, was delegated to establish a mission for the
Indigenous west of the Sault, between Green Bay,
Wisconsin, and Lake Superior. For this purpose, he
left Québec with the Ottawas, who had paddled
from Lake Superior to Québec with Radisson and
Groseilliers and were now making their return trip
home.

Father Charles Albanel, Jean Guerin, and six
other Frenchmen went along for the trip. It is
disappointing that those six men were not named
in *Jesuit Relations*.

For a voyageur or a coureur de bois, it was
enough just to get through the lengthy, strenuous
workday, never mind keep a journal. As a result,
not everyone was documented.

The Ottawas were the first Indigenous group
from the upper Great Lakes to trade with the
French, therefore, their homeland became known
by the French traders and priests as the Ottawa
country.

On his way to the intended mission site in the
Ottawa country, Father Ménard passed through
the Sault, continuing on to stay with the Indigenous
at Keweenaw Bay (basically southeast of Houghton,
MI) over the winter. Once there, he made himself
as comfortable as he could in a crudely constructed
cabin, made of fir boughs. Not long after settling in,
he realized that the Indigenous were not fond of
his presence.

Not wanting his religious zest to be wasted, he turned his attention to a group of Hurons who had arrived in an effort to avoid contact with the Iroquois, who were again on the war path.

Once spring arrived, he proceeded on to Chequamegon Bay, north of present day Ashland, Wisconsin.

During the summer, while making his way toward the Indigenous, who he had been told were starving at Lac Courte Oreilles (in northcentral Wisconsin) he became separated from his sole travelling companion at a portage and died. Although the exact details of his death are unknown, it is believed that he died during the middle of August of 1661, when he portaged rapids on the Rib River, northwest of what is now Wausau, Wisconsin.

Eventually, the Sioux found his breviary and cassock and placed them on the alter where they prayed to the Great Spirit.

Census Taking

The census of 1660 in Québec showed 3,418 people, with the majority of them at Québec City, and others at Trois-Rivières and Montreal, with many of those listed as having been born in New France, now Canada.

Incidentally, during this year alone, the warring Iroquois killed seventy of the French settlers.

As this census did not include the Indigenous, we can see that there was a vast number of Indigenous people in Canada compared to the French.

As an aside, my 9th great-grandparents, Mathurin Chabot and Marie Mésange, were married in Notre-Dame de Québec, at Québec City, on November 17, 1661.

In 1662, Iroquois Point was again the scene of a battle.

A hunting group of Ojibway, Chippewa, Ottawas, Nipissings and Anikouets, were returning from the west, according to *Jesuit Relations,* when they saw smoke at the entrance to Whitefish Bay [near Sault Ste. Marie, Michigan].

Once again, the Iroquois were in their backyard. Scouts checked the area, noting about one hundred Iroquois.

While the Iroquois were sleeping, near daybreak, about one hundred Indigenous attacked them by firstly firing their muskets and secondly by shooting arrows. They then leaped on any Iroquois who was not yet dead and continued attacking with hatchets. The Iroquois were prevented from running away because the arrows were coming at them fast and furious from all directions. The battle concluded with only a few Iroquois escaping.

Fowle related a different version that was orally told throughout history. It goes that the Iroquois started off winning, killing many men, and taking large numbers of prisoners.

Those who survived managed to leave the fray in their canoes and headed across the bay to Gros Cap (west of present-day Sault Ste. Marie, Ontario).

During the night they saw the fires at Whitefish and quietly paddled back.

Just at the break of day, they attacked the sleeping Iroquois. Only a few Iroquois survived. The only man killed from the Ojibway side was one who was hit by a flying awl, thrown by an elderly woman, sitting at the opening to a wigwam.

An awl is a pointed object used to repair moccasins.

It may seem strange that an elderly woman was with the Iroquois, but throughout history, the warriors did take their relatives with them when they left their home turf to wage war.

The King Steps In

In 1665, the Marquis de Tracy arrived in Québec, as lieutenant-general, along with the first detachment of troops, being the Carignan-Salières Regiment, which quickly put down the Iroquois in 1666.

By 1667, the Iroquois agreed to a peace agreement with the French that lasted for 20 years.

Once peace was attained with the Iroquois both, what is now, Canada and the United States began to flourish.

Pictographs

These Indigenous paintings were created during the 17th and 18th centuries.

Chief Shingwauk of Garden River may have created some of the paintings that signify important details of Ojibway history. Some likely depict war of the past, especially against the Iroquois.

The paintings, on a steep rock face beside Lake Superior, were created by using ochre, which is a natural clay pigment, made of ferric oxide with differing amounts of clay mixed with sand. The resulting colours can be red, orange, brown, or yellow. Red ochre was mixed with fish oil and animal grease and painted on white crystalline granite.

Thor Conway in his book, *Spirits on Stone, Lake Superior Ojibway History, Legends and the Agawa Pictographs,* provides much detail regarding these pictographs. He also reported that the granite secrets a clear mineral fluid that acts as a natural varnish.

Anishinaabe pictographs can be seen at Agawa Bay, off Trans-Canada Highway 17, a little more than 80 miles (134 km) north of the Sault.

Sturdy shoes are highly recommended as the hike into the area is treacherous.

Agawa Bay Pictographs

by Sheri Minardi Photography

Father Claude Allouez wrote that he, along with several Frenchmen (two of whom were called La tour and Nicolas) and a few hundred Indigenous from various nations, left Trois-Rivières [Quebec] on August 8, 1665.

The priest wrote: "we reached the Sault, for such is the name given to half a league of rapids that are encountered in a beautiful river which unites two great lakes, that of the Hurons and Lake Superior."

They wanted to stay at the Sault to get to know the few Frenchmen living there, but after a few days, they continued on before Lake Superior's waves turned violent. Again, it is unfortunate that the names of these Frenchmen were not recorded.

Allouez further wrote: "on the second of September, then, after clearing this Sault . . . we entered Lake Superior, which will henceforth bear Monsieur de Tracy's name; in recognition to him on the part of the people of those regions." He was referring to the Indigenous people being grateful that peace with the Iroquois had been accomplished by de Tracy and his troops.

He further wrote that the Anishinaabe "revere this lake as a divinity, and offer it sacrifice whether on account of its size...or on account of its goodness in furnishing fish for the sustenance of their tribes, in default of game which is scarce in the neighborhood."

The priest went on to explain that pure copper was found at the bottom of Lake Superior. He noted that the Anishinaabe thought of the copper as a divinity, or as presents that the gods living under the water gave to them. The Anishinaabe took care of the copper pieces forever and passed them down through their families as inheritances.

Father Alloüez constructed a bark chapel at his destination of Chequamegon Bay. This was a bit south of the where Father Ménard had been, and not far from where Radisson had built a hut, four years prior. The mission became known as La Pointe which attracted Hurons and Algonquins to settle there, to avoid the Iroquois.

The priests were always welcomed by the Indigenous people but it seems more than anything that the priests were curiosities, especially their religious ceremonies.

Alloüez returned to Quebec, but on August 6, 1667, he left there, with Father Louis Nicolas returning to the Sault, followed by La Pointe.

Alloüez wrote in *Jesuit Relations* in 1667 that he had given Catholic religious instruction at the Sault "on various occasions, but especially when I sojourned with them . . . for a whole month." At that time, in addition to baptizing an adult who was dying, he baptized twenty children. It was thought that he was there to assist Father Miedas but there is no proof that Father Miedas was present over that winter, and in fact, I have found no references regarding him at all.

Father Louis Nicolas

On Upon his arrival at the Sault with Allouez, Nicolas remained. It has been suggested that he attempted to start a mission, but I suspect that it was unlikely, given he left in the spring of 1668.

I noticed that not much was mentioned about him in *Jesuit Relations*. Now I know why. He was considered to be the black sheep of the Jesuits because he was more interested in writing and drawing sketches of Indigenous people and nature than converting anyone to Christianity.

When he did interact with the Indigenous people, his behavior toward them was not at all Christian.

It is not known why he came to the Sault, except that he liked to travel, but perhaps it was because he was an expert in the Algonquin language.

Apparently, he believed that he was in the West Indies so that his manuscript is entitled *Histoire Naturelle des Indes Occidentales*. It describes plants, birds, fish, and Indigenous people of New France, and his *Codex canadenses* illustrates those subjects. [The word codex, now an obsolete word, simply means a manuscript in book form.]

After he returned to France, he tried to have his work published, but the Vatican would not hear of it, with the result that Nicolas quit the priesthood.

An interesting article about Father Nicolas was written by Brian Bethune, in Macleans Magazine on November 21, 2011. After more than three centuries, in an indirect way, Nicolas has a book out.

Eventually, Concordia University Art Historian, François-Marc Gagnon, spent thirty years researching the work and determined that Louis Nicolas had created it. In November, 2011, McGill Queen's University Press released *The Codex Canadensis and The Writings of Louis Nicolas*, which is 550-pages.

Ermatinger-Clergue National Historic Site

Display at Sault Ste. Marie, ON

The priests felt that the Sault would be the best area to establish another mission because it was the focal point of the three upper Great Lakes. Perhaps the best of all reasons was that there was a permanent Indigenous village which attracted many hundreds of other Indigenous people for social visits, trading, and fishing. As a bonus, French fur traders and coureurs de bois were established at the Sault to trade with the Indigenous.

Father François Joseph Mercier wrote in *Jesuit Relations* on April 21, 1668 that several priests were going "up the river" meaning the river at the Sault. One of them was Father Jacques Marquette who arrived that summer.

It is believed that he established a permanent mission here. Marquette found that the local Indigenous wanted to be baptized. He was reluctant to do so because he had concerns that they would return to their own beliefs.

After one year, Marquette moved on to Chequamegon where the Ottawas bluntly rejected the priests.

Marquette replaced Allöuez at La Pointe in 1669, but he was not there very long before the Sioux, from the west, caused aggravation.

As a result, in 1670, Marquette conducted a move by these Indigenous to a new mission at Point St. Ignace.

It was from Point St. Ignace, on May 17, 1673, that Marquette left with Louis Jolliet for the Mississippi River.

Father Dablon wrote in *Jesuit Relations* of 1669-70: "Therefore we have been obliged to establish here a permanent Mission, which we call Sainte Marie du Sault..."

It is not clear which priest chose this name, or perhaps the name was a joint decision, and there has been some discussion as to which priest founded this mission.

Fowle explained that three different priests were credited with it between 1668 and 1670.

With Marquette's departure from the Sault, Father Claude Dablon arrived in 1669, as superior of the Ottawa mission, and made the Sault his headquarters, but he soon left to travel around Lake Superior with Father Alloüez.

Incidentally, his travels resulted in a nearly exact map of that lake, referred to as the Carte des Jésuits. It also showed the upper portions of lakes Michigan and Huron.

Apart from his zeal for exploration and the teaching of Christianity, Dablon took a firm stand against providing liquor to the Indigenous, which he accomplished with much tact.

Dablon's stay turned out to be short because he was appointed superior of all the Jesuit missions in Canada so that he returned to Quebec in 1671.

Perhaps the basis of the mission at the Sault was started during, or before 1668; however, there are historical writers who state that it was built in 1669. One of them was William W. Warren, an eloquent Indigenous historian who wrote in 1850; the other reference was by two Sulpitian priests who visited the mission.

In May, 1670, the Sulpitian priests, René de Brehant de Galinée and François Dollier de Casson, arrived at the Sault for a brief stay.

Regarding the priests and the mission at the Sault, their report stated, "they have two men in their service since last year, who have built them a pretty fort." This would suggest that the mission was built in 1669. These priests mentioned the stockade, house, chapel, and referred to the priests' vegetable garden and that they were expecting to bake bread within a few years.

Around the mission was a stockade made of twelve-foot high cedar poles, and within the stockade was a cabin for the priests, along with a chapel.

Outside the stockade, to the south and east, the priests tended a garden, and cleared fields to grow wheat. They had expected that this would encourage the Indigenous to remain in one place but such was not the case.

From *Jesuit Relations*, we know that the mission was located at the foot of the rapids on what is now the American side of the river, slightly beneath the 46th latitude degree.

Bernie Arbic, of Sault, Michigan, in his book, *City of the Rapids: Sault Ste. Marie's Heritage* wrote: "the mission was located approximately at the intersection of present-day Water Street and Bingham Ave."

According to Fowle, the Federal building grounds and the area south of Portage Avenue are where the garden and fields had been.

It was interesting that Galinée and Casson commented that the Jesuits' main influence was with the twenty to twenty-five French who were there. I was surprised to learn that there were so many Frenchmen at the Sault in 1670, and again, it is disappointing that no names were recorded.

These visiting priests saw no Christianity among the Indigenous people. They thought it was "extraordinary" that the Jesuits were baptizing Indigenous people before they understood what the Catholic religion was about.

Father Claude Dablon, in *Jesuit Relations* of 1669-1670, described the art of fishing at the Sault. He basically stated that not everyone could fish in the rapids because some, by the vigorous handling of the pole, flipped the canoe. The task could not be done unless the fisherman was strong as well as agile. He had to keep his balance while standing in the canoe, in the midst of whirlpools. In his hands was a pole with a net on one end that was shaped like a pocket. He needed serious concentration to follow the fish as they moved among the rocks - keep his eyes on them - then thrust his net in a particular way to capture them - then with a sudden, strong pull, he raised the net, flipping the fish into the canoe.

Normally, he caught six to seven large fish at a single dipping of the pole. He continued until he had the canoe filled with fish. I would imagine that the birch bark canoe must have been exceptionally constructed to withstand the turbulent rapids.

During the summer of 1670 there was a severe epidemic; however, the Jesuits reported that the Indigenous people who gave the teachings of Christianity their undivided attention were not affected by the epidemic and filled the church.

It is not my intent to put the Jesuits down, but I think it is noteworthy that the priests did not report how many Indigenous people did die from the epidemic.

Jesuit Relations further reported that on October 11th of that year, the Indigenous elders declared to the priests that everyone in the village was now Christian.

Voyageurs at Dawn

Painting by Frances Anne Hopkins (1838 – 1919)
Created December 31, 1870.
Library and Archives Canada, Acc. No. 1989-401-3

By 1670, there was pressure for the French in that the English were now commercially advancing in the north with the Hudson's Bay Company.

On the American eastern seaboard, the English were progressing with agriculture and manufacturing.

These two situations caused France to stake its claim for sovereignty in the interior.

Simon François Daumont, Sieur de Saint Lusson, along with Nicolas Perrot, Louis Jolliet, the Mississippi explorer, and four Jesuit priests, being Louis André, Gabriel Dreuillettes, Claude Dablon, and Claude Alloüez, went to Manitoulin Island, Ontario, during the fall of 1670, spending the winter there while contemplating the upcoming pageant to be held at the Sault.

Father Louis André, who had arrived in Québec in 1669, came to the mission at the Sault during the summer of 1670 with Father Gabriel Druillettes, who taught André the Indigenous culture.

During 1670-71, except during the winter when he stayed on Manitoulin Island, André lived with some Ottawas, who had moved to Chequamegon Bay on southern Lake Superior, near present day Ashland, Wisconsin, to escape the Iroquois.

In 1671, Father André returned to the Sault for the pageant, and then moved on to Green Bay, Wisconsin, for the next twelve years devoting his teachings to the Menominees until 1683 when he was called to Saint Ignace, Michigan, returning to Québec a year later.

Father Alloüez was highly respected by the Indigenous people perhaps because he so eloquently spoke their languages fluently.

He travelled Lakes Erie, Huron, Michigan, and Superior, covering a distance of approximately 3,000 miles, and is credited with having baptized about 10,000 people during his twenty-four years among twenty-three different Indigenous nations, prior to his death in August, 1689.

Father Gabriel Dreuillettes arrived in Québec, from France, in 1643, and proceeded to have an incredible career in both Canada and the U.S.A., covering vast areas. It is not commonly known, but Father Dreuillettes was the priest who initiated the plan to establish missions in the west as early as 1655. He based his idea on reports provided by Radisson and Groseilliers, as well as accounts he obtained from the Indigenous people at Tadoussac.

Father Dreuillettes studied the locations and numbers of the various nations in the west.

In 1656, he did strike out towards the west with some Algonquins but, because he was abandoned by them, he had to turn back.

In 1661, he again tried to fulfill his plan, but this time he proceeded via Tadoussac, Quebec, the Saguenay, and Hudson Bay, with Father Claude Dablon. Along the way, although they were a long way from the Iroquois, his Indigenous guides quit the journey and returned to Tadoussac, due to their fear of potential Iroquois attacks.

It was not until 1670, at the age of sixty, with a worn out, stiff-jointed body, but with amazing courage and zeal, that he finally got to the mission at the Sault and took charge. He was the Jesuit who made the strongest impression on the Indigenous people because of his zeal, gentle ways, and his ability to work miracles for them. Each year there was a report in *Jesuit Relations* as to his accomplishments at the Sault.

He was noted for his inspiration of other priests, including Charles Albanel, Jacques Marquette, Claude Dablon, and Henri Nouvel.

It is not clear when Father Henri Nouvel was at the Sault but he wrote in *Jesuit Relations* that he left the Sault on October 31, 1671, to travel through the missions north of Lake Huron.

Perhaps he arrived at the Sault after the pageant had been held, given he was not mentioned as one of the priests in attendance.

Later, in 1677, he received the remains of Father Marquette and buried them in the mission chapel near Point Saint Ignace at the head of East Moran Bay.

From Manitoulin Island, Ontario, runners were sent out during the early spring of 1671 to encourage the Indigenous people, within a radius of more than 300 miles (500 km) of the Sault, that an important ceremony would take place at the Sault on June 14 of that year.

It is believed that more than 2,000 Indigenous people, including the Winnebago, Menominee, Potawatomi, Sauk, from what is now the United States, as well as the various Canadian Algonquins nations and Cree began arriving during May for the ceremony.

The reasons for having the ceremony at the Sault were described by Father Claude Dablon in *Jesuit Relations* of 1671-1672. He basically stated that the Sault was the water crossroad for both the Indigenous people and the French. It was on the route of all who travelled to Québec with furs from a vast area. In addition, it was a meeting place where numerous Indigenous nations converged to fish and visit.

Before the pageant, Lusson, Perrot, Jolliet, and Fathers André, Dreuillettes, Dablon, and Allouëz moved from Manitoulin Island to the Sault.

The Pageant of St. Lusson on June 14, 1671

The ceremony, also known as the Pageant of the Sault, was translated to the Indigenous people by Nicolas. Louis Jolliet was one of fifteen to twenty Frenchmen who signed the official document declaring France's ownership of the land. It is believed that also present was Mathurin Cadeau, whose son was Jean Baptiste Cadotte, but we will get to him a little later. Another undocumented attendee is believed to have been Jean Péré. The four Jesuit priests previously described were also in attendance.

The ceremony took place on the south side of the St. Marys River, on the hill overlooking the Indigenous village and the Jesuit mission. In the background were giant green pine trees and in front was the St. Marys River.

Leading the procession from the mission up the hill to the location of the ceremony were the priests, in their black robes, carrying crucifixes, while singing a Latin hymn. Next came the French traders, including Perrot. Bringing up the end was Lusson, dressed in the uniform of a French officer, carrying his sword overhead.

On the hill stood the Indigenous people with their calumets, which were long stemmed tobacco peace pipes.

The cross was blessed by Father Claude Dablon, and when it had been raised, the Vexilla [hymn] was sung.

Father Dablon's description of the ceremony was that the Frenchmen joined the priests in singing the hymn, and the Indigenous people were impressed. Next, a shield depicting the French coat of arms, on a cedar pole, was raised above the cross. While this was being done, the Exaudiat was sung, followed by a prayer for the King. While Lusson was proclaiming the lands to be the King's possessions, the French shouted: "Long live the King" at the same time that muskets were fired.

Of course, the Indigenous people were impressed because they had never before witnessed such pomp and ceremony.

Father Alloüez then eulogized the French King. Again, the Indigenous people were impressed because they had no idea that there was one person who was so great, not to mention wealthy and powerful.

Lusson then stated to the Indigenous people in "martial and eloquent language" that he was taking the land for the French King and that they would be protected by him. The ceremony was concluded with a bonfire and the singing of the Te Deum.

Lusson had formally claimed for the King of France all lands already discovered and lands yet to be discovered in all directions to the seas of the north, west, and south. Basically, he had claimed all lands in North America that were not already occupied by the English.

The entire speech about the king was such over the top exaggeration that the Indigenous people could not help but be in awe of him.

There are no details as to how the approval of fourteen Indigenous Nations was acquired except that the speakers at the ceremony were eloquent and persuasive.

According to Nicholas Perrot, in Parkman Club Papers, and as noted by Fowle, as soon as the French were not looking, the Indigenous people hauled down the arms of France, promptly melted the lead from the seal, and created bullets for their guns. So much for sovereignty.

There were reports that the cross was pulled down; however, other reports state that it remained for a long time, on the hill near the Indigenous burial ground.

Two weeks after the Pageant, on June 27, 1671, the Jesuit mission at the Sault burned. No one knows why.

Jesuit Relations reported that a much better chapel was constructed, following which, twenty-six children were baptized, all within one day. Was this because the Indigenous people were in awe of the beauty of the new chapel? The priests continued to report that the Indigenous people were experiencing miracles and they expected, very soon, that the Indigenous people would become as civilized as they were.

The priests wrote that, by 1672, the Indigenous people were planting corn and bringing their harvests to them. Father Dreuillettes' response was to sprinkle holy water and pray over the fields, but there was a reason why the Indigenous people congregated at the mission. It was a safe haven for them from the Sioux. They feared the Sioux, and at the same time, were of the opinion that the priests' prayers could protect them. For some unknown reason, making peace with the Sioux did not cross their minds.

Louis Jolliet

Jolliet engaged in a fur trading business, along with others, to finance the trip he planned to make down the Mississippi River. It was at the Sault where he conducted that trade with the Anishinaabe for furs.

It has been claimed that he spent the winter of 1672-1673 at the Sault engaging in the fur trade, but he may have been at the Sault for part of the time, and at St. Ignace with Father Marquette for some of the winter, given they were preparing for their trip. He really did not need to be at the Sault because his brother, Zacharie, along with others of Jolliet's partners, were here looking after the fur business. Zacharie did not accompany his brother on the trip down the Mississippi but stayed at the Sault to continue on their fur trade.

In May of 1673, Jolliet set off from St. Ignace for the Mississippi but returned to the Sault for the winter of 1673-1674 where he worked on writing a copy of his logbook and map which when completed were left with the priests. These copies that he left with the Jesuits at the Sault were destroyed when the priests' house burned in the spring of 1674.

Unfortunately, his original logbook and map were later lost when his canoe capsized in Québec. Jolliet recounted his adventure from memory but there were gaps which were never filled in.

It is believed that the best account of his journey was written by Father Claude Dablon.

Cree v. Sioux

Although the Sioux had enormous skill at war, some of the Anishinaabe from the Sault invaded the Sioux and managed to capture eighty of their warriors. This is not the first time that we have heard about the Ojibway/Chippewa skills in assaulting their enemies.

With this in mind, in the spring of 1674, ten Sioux warriors arrived at the Sault for the purpose of arranging a peaceful settlement.

The problem was that there were Cree visiting the Sault at the time, and because they were sworn enemies of the Sioux, they were not going to allow a peace treaty. The Cree made it known that they were going to kill the Sioux.

Both Fathers Dablon and Dreuillettes were at the mission, but it was Father Dreuillettes who gave the Sioux protection in the mission house, on the understanding that they would be amenable to his teachings of Christianity.

Meanwhile, other Indigenous people crowded around the outside of the mission house. Some of them were in favour of peace while others were not.

Attempts were made to ensure that everyone who entered the mission house was disarmed but given the confusion, about six Cree gained entry with their knives. One of them insulted a Sioux and the fight was on.

The Sioux thought that the Ojibway/Chippewa and the Cree had joined together in a plan to kill them all. As the other Indigenous people present were without arms, the Sioux managed to kill some of them, while the remainder fled.

Those who fled quickly gathered up their arms and returned to the fight.

At the same time, the Sioux blocked the door to the house; found guns stored in the house and proceeded to fire out through the windows.

On the outside, Indigenous people piled straw and birch bark canoes against the house and lit them on fire.

At this point, the Sioux hightailed it out of the house, grabbed stakes that been holding up a hut, and continued to fight.

Father Dreuillettes wrote: "It was a horrible spectacle to see so many slaughtered and so much blood shed in so small a space."

The result was that the priests had lost their home and forty Ojibway/Chippewa and Crees were either injured or killed. The ten Sioux, along with two women who had accompanied them, were killed.

The Ojibway/Chippewa deserted the mission out of fear that other Sioux would soon arrive.

I can only assume that the priests must have been very grateful that this did not happen.

The year of 1674 did not go well at the mission but at least the chapel was saved, and at some point, a third mission house was built.

Father Dablon wrote in *Jesuit Relations* regarding the year 1675 that Father Henri Nouvel was the superior at "Sainte Marie," where he was assisted by Father Gabriel Dreuillettes, whose "great age and infirmities did not in the least diminish his zeal," and by Father Bailoquet, who came to the Sault from time to time.

War had been ongoing for many years at Chequamegon where the Sioux fought with the Hurons and Ottawas. No doubt this made the area dangerous for the fur traders.

The Sault, being the place where the traders met, was too close to Chequamegon for comfort, although they continued to trade in the area between the Sault and Chequamegon.

To placate the Indigenous people, Governor Frontenac sent Hugues Randin to the Sault in 1676 with gifts from the government to be given to the Sioux. His goal was to create peace with the Sioux, as well as friendly relations among them and the fur traders. Apparently, he was successful in his endeavours.

Father Dreuillettes was the superior at the Sault during 1677-1678; however, his already precarious health was further failing. Therefore, in about 1679, with ten active years' service to his credit at the Sault, he was taken back to Québec, where he died within about one year.

Between the years 1679 and 1696, the Jesuits did not document much of the activities at the Sault. They wrote that Father Charles Albanel was appointed superior of the Ottawa missions, in 1679, and therefore, moved from de Père, near Green Bay, Wisconsin, to the Sault, where he shared responsibility of the mission with Father Louis André.

At some unreported point, Father de la Tour arrived and was here at least during 1683.

The mission was an active place where, in addition to the Ojibway/Chippewa, other Indigenous people, including the Cree, came.

On January 11, 1696 at the age of eighty years, Father Albanel died at the Sault. I assume he was buried there but I am not aware of a monument to his memory.

It is possible that the mission at the Sault closed upon the death of Father Albanel in early 1696. Fowle mentioned that there are no records of any other priest living at the Sault "for the next hundred years and more."

When Quaife researched the question as to the closure of the Sault mission, all he could find was that the closure likely happened between 1694 and 1700.

Fowle noted, "Father Sagard, in his writing, first tried to fix upon the village by the falls the name Sault du Gaston…" Whether this name was Sagard's idea or Brûlé's, or someone else's, we do not know. Fowle pointed out that there was a letter written to the Reverend Father Provincial of France by Father Thierry Beschefur, Superior in Canada, on October 21, 1683, wherein, for the first time, the Sault was referred to as Sault De Ste. Marie. It was Fowle's idea that the name evolved over time rather than having been chosen by someone.

Further, Fowle wrote that once the Jesuits had established their mission, they referred to it as Sainte Marie du Sault or the Sault between the years 1668 and 1683.

Alexander Henry in 1762 and onward wrote about it as the Sault de Sainte-Marie.

It appears that it was about 1683 when our name came to be what it is now, except that at some later point "de" was dropped.

I did notice, during the early nineteenth century, the writers of letters sent to the Sault, referred to it as Ste. Marie's.

Heroes of the Wilderness

In French, the word 'coureur' means runner and the word 'bois' means wood, as in forest, trees, and bush. This hero of the wilderness wore a blanket coat. On his feet were moose hide moccasins. His leggings were made from deer skins. Always a cap was on his head and a red sash across his chest.

A job posting for a coureur de bois would state,

Must be:
Accustomed to hardship, difficulty, pain, and cold;
Physically and mentally tough;
Able to deal with danger;
A natural diplomat;
Proficient in determining direction;
An expert canoe handler and repairer;
An adept scout;
Ability to learn second language;
Experienced in trapping animals;
Able to distinguish good furs and their value;
Able to negotiate;
A survivor of any weather condition; and
Able to continue when threatened with starvation.
Only those with these qualifications need apply.

There were no postings for the job.
A man, whatever his background, just made the decision to travel by canoe into the wilderness

and taught himself the trade and how to survive in it.

He led the way for others, following behind him, to manage cultural differences attendant to life among the Indigenous people.

He married into the Indigenous nations and his children were accepted and protected by their Indigenous relatives.   Today, they are called Métis.

He opened trade with the Indigenous people and kept it operating through political changes within the country.

He kept the peace between various Indigenous nations and, in time, he became the leader who negotiated settlement of issues between the government and the Indigenous people.

He worked so very hard and endured endless dangers, over thousands of miles, to acquire furs.

Trading companies wanted him to work for them but could not give him protection during his treacherous travels, and provided no danger pay.

Benefits of any kind were unheard of.

Painting by Cornelius Krieghoff
(Dutch-Canadian 1815 – 1872)
McCord Museum, Montreal, Quebec

By his government, he was considered to be a criminal and a rebel. It wanted to share in his profits but provided him with nothing in return. Unless he had acquired a licence from his government, he was considered to be an illegitimate trader, and if found out, he faced confiscation of his furs, was fined, and served jail time.

The fur trade was the industry that kept Canada on solid economic ground but the coureurs de bois, instead of being held in high esteem, had to live underground. There was an official report in 1680 that showed that 800 men out of a population of 10,000 were unaccountable and presumed to be coureurs de bois.

When operating without a licence, he could not go back to his family in Québec. He lived among the Indigenous people and experienced such freedom that he had no desire to resume life in Québec as a farmer, fisherman, or storekeeper.

To avoid sharing his profits with the powers that were in Québec, he sold furs to the English and Dutch along the east coast. By doing so, he got better prices for his furs.

Not all of them were considered to be outlaws. Some acquired licences and paid taxes to their government. This type of man was welcomed home when he arrived with furs and was celebrated. He was called a voyageur.

Alexander Henry described the diet of a coureur de bois. Maize, also known as Indian corn, was boiled in strong lye, then the husk was removed. Finally, it was mashed, dried, and fried like rice. Every person was allotted one quart per day. For a month, a bushel, with two pounds of fat, was considered to be enough for a man. Nothing else was taken but the men stayed healthy.

Alexander Henry thought that no one, other than the French Canadians, could follow this diet so that the fur trade monopoly was theirs.

Incidentally, the duration of an average round trip between the Ottawa country and Montreal was sixteen months.

This brings us to the most well-known coureur de bois of them all – Du Luth.

Daniel Greysolon, Sieur Du Luth, for which the city of Duluth is named, arrived in the Sault during the fall of 1678, with a crew of seven voyageurs, to winter here.

Once the ice had melted on the river in the spring, he and his group headed west along the south shore of Lake Superior.

After various adventures, Du Luth took command of Michilimackinac in 1683.

That summer, he was told that two Frenchmen, Jacques Le Maire and Colin Berthot, had left the Sault to trade with the Indians at Keweenaw. Finally, we have the names of some Frenchmen who were at the Sault in the seventeenth century.

While at Keweenaw, they were robbed and murdered, purportedly by Achiganaga, an Ottawa chief, his sons, and a Menominee.

To ensure that the French could be kept safe, Du Luth decided to set an example. He sent Jean Péré, and a few others, to track down the murderers and arrest them.

Péré, who was considered to be an excellent scout, had been sent by Intendant Talon sixteen years prior to look for the copper mines. Somehow, he lost interest in copper and took to trading for furs.

Meanwhile, fifteen Saulteur families had fled Chequamegon because they believed that the Sioux were about to retaliate against them for an attack they had made on the Sioux during the previous spring. The Menominee fellow went with them to the mission at the Sault.

On October 24, 1683, Du Luth heard that the wanted Menominee was now at the Sault.

The twelve Frenchmen who resided at the Sault knew the wanted Menominee was there but did not dare to arrest him because they were afraid of Indigenous reprisals against them.

Du Luth decided to take action so that the next day, he left for the Sault, accompanied by seven Frenchmen.

Once they were about one and one-half miles below the Sault, Du Luth and three others, left their canoe and walked through the forest, along the shore, near the line of what is now Portage Avenue. The others continued on by canoe.

Du Luth quietly approached the mission, arrested the Menominee, and arranged to have six men guard him.

Meanwhile, Péré, with the help of eighteen Frenchmen, had arrested Achiganaga's entire family, which was the normal procedure at that time.

The chief's sons admitted to what they had done and described to Péré where the stolen goods were hid. With this information, Péré found the goods as well as the bodies of the murdered Frenchmen. Any goods that had not been ruined were auctioned off to the traders.

Then, twelve coureurs de bois who were wintering at Keweenaw, helped Péré bring the prisoners to the Sault.

Upon arrival, the prisoners were guarded in the house where Du Luth was staying, while not being permitted to speak to each other. How they accomplished this in a small house, I do not know.

On November 26, Du Luth began a council, which followed the normal French rules of a court proceeding. Each accused was allowed to have two relatives to defend him. They were individually questioned and their answers were put in writing and read back to them, with an opportunity to correct the record, if necessary.

Chiefs and other important Indigenous people who attended the hearing found it extremely interesting.

In due course, Achiganaga was cleared of the charges against him. The others were convicted by a jury of their peers, being the chiefs who were present.

There were still some protests from the Indigenous people regarding the planned execution of the convicted men. Du Luth maintained that because they had murdered, they must die in the same manner as the Frenchmen had, but he agreed that it would be two men who would be put to death so that it would be man for man, and that those two men should be Achiganaga's oldest son and the Menominee. The superior of the mission, De la tour, agreed with Du Luth.

The priests then baptized the condemned men and thereafter, led by Du Luth, forty-two Frenchmen walked up a hill with the prisoners and, in view of about four hundred Indigenous people, the two men were shot.

Fowle explained that the execution took place on the same hill, situated south of the Weitzel lock, where twelve years earlier, St. Lusson had planted a cross. It was Fowle's thinking that it could not have been Ashmun Hill because that was too great a distance for the prisoners to be taken, especially considering that area was thick with trees, and about four hundred hostile Indigenous people were watching.

Later, Nicholas Perrot took over command of Michilimackinac from Du Luth.

As for Du Luth, his dream of finding a route to the western sea was overshadowed by other distractions, so that he never got back to his intended quest.

Fighting the Iroquois Again

Five years later, in September of 1688, Baron de La Hontan visited the Sault to approach forty Saulteur warriors to join in his campaign against the Iroquois to the south.

La Hontan wrote about the Sault, ". . . not far from the Jesuit's house, there is a village of Outchipouis [Chippewas] alias Saulteurs. This place is a thoroughfare for the coureurs de bois that trade with the northern people."

The Saulteurs agreed to fight with Lahontan and in that regard, he wrote, "The Saulteurs came off with honor, for they lost only four men, and of the twenty Iroquois, they killed three, wounded five and took the rest prisoners so that not one of them escaped."

Again, we see that the Saulteurs have not lost their touch when dealing with the Iroquois.

Why Did the Sault Decline?

From about 1671, war between the Sioux and the Saulteurs and their allies was underway. Lake Superior had become a dangerous place to be for both the Indigenous people and the French.

We already know that the atmosphere at La Pointe had become so dangerous that Father Marquette had relocated the Indigenous people from La Pointe to Point St. Ignace, being at the Straits of Mackinac, in Lake Michigan.

As a result, the fur trade and missionary work began to gradually centre in that area.

Then, during the early 1680s when the Iroquois renewed their warfare, Mackinac became the military centre.

So, it appears that the war with the Iroquois led to the eventual abandonment of the Mission at the Sault.

As a result of the explorations of Jolliet, in 1673, along the Mississippi, followed by La Salle, in 1682, France proclaimed ownership of the Mississippi Valley which opened up that area for the French fur traders.

By 1689, war had begun between France and England so that reinforcements were sent by the French to Mackinac in an effort to improve the Indigenous loyalty to France.

It did take considerable time, but peace was restored in 1697.

In 1694, because the Iroquois were still fiercely waging war, Antoine Lamothe Cadillac was appointed commandant at Mackinac where he stayed for three years.

Unfortunately, church and state collided because Cadillac and the Jesuit priests intensely disapproved of each other's ideals.

On April 25, 1696, the French King issued orders that all of the French, except the priests, had to evacuate the area.

This turned out to be a major mistake because the Indigenous people, to save travelling to Québec with their furs, proceeded to trade with the English who began moving into the area.

Eighteenth Century

1700 Shake Up

In an attempt to prevent a takeover by the English, Cadillac arranged to move to the St. Clair and Detroit Rivers which would provide a center to control the upper country. While establishing a fort at Detroit in 1701, Cadillac encouraged the Indigenous of the upper lakes to move there, which many did.

From this point on, activity at both the Sault and Michilimackinac was on the downslide. Even the Jesuits left the upper lakes for a while.

We can see that the Sault had been the place to be for both the fur traders and the missionaries because it was a meeting place of a few thousand Indigenous people.

Further, on account of its location, the residents could easily notice who was approaching them.

Then the focus moved to Michilimackinac because of Indigenous wars.

Next, because of Cadillac, and his establishment of Detroit, the focus shifted to that location.

There is not much information as to what was happening at the Sault in the early eighteenth century.

Were the Indigenous people still meeting at the rapids? It was likely but without the Jesuit presence, nothing was documented.

By 1712, the French at Detroit were embroiled in a war with the Fox of Wisconsin which war was almost as dreadful as the war with the Iroquois.

The Fox war caused uproar in the upper Great Lakes for the next twenty-five years or more.

Control of the route to Wisconsin was via the Straits of Mackinac so that, in 1715, a garrison was established at what is now Mackinac City.

Eventually, in 1781, a new fort on Mackinac Island replaced it.

Less than twenty years after being ordered out, the French began moving back into the upper Great Lakes, establishing military posts, situated to control the fur trade, but none was located at the Sault. There was one post at Mackinac and another at Green Bay.

The third post, at Chequamegon, was the only one that would have any influence on the Sault. It had been abandoned in 1697 but was restored in 1718. The reason for reoccupying this area was to control the Saulteurs from engaging in war against the Foxes in Wisconsin. It also guarded people against the Sioux to the west. Perhaps because there was a military presence at Chequamegon, it replaced the Sault as the center of Indigenous activity. As well, the French still had not given up on finding the way to the Orient that they thought was west of Chequamegon.

Louis Denys de la Ronde

Louis Denys de la Ronde became the commandant at Chequamegon, in 1727, and was granted the right to fur trade there, but was unable to take up this command until 1731.

Soon after arriving, he found out from the Indigenous people that there was copper in the area. His focus then became to prospect copper to make his fortune.

A proposal was made to the government whereby he would have a twenty-five-ton ship constructed to sail on Lake Superior in exchange for a free nine-year lease on the fur trade, which he was granted, to finance the cost of the ship.

Materials, along with the work force, came from Montreal.

During 1734, a shipyard was constructed at Pointe aux Pins, just above the Sault, on the Canadian side, with the ship being built the same year.

In 1736, La Ronde had some small samples of copper from the Ontonagon River sent to France for evaluation. The French report was positive as to its value.

Two German mineral experts arrived at the Sault by canoe, in June of 1738, and then went on to examine copper at a few locations.

It was not until early summer of 1739 when they reported that the copper was good quality but the enterprise would be too costly to process.

Following this, La Ronde hired twelve carpenters and sawyers who were living at the Sault, sending them to Chequamegon.

Perhaps they were fur traders who also had these skills as it seems unlikely that such skilled tradesmen would have been working at the Sault.

By 1740, La Ronde was advised by the government that his project was not to be. Ultimately, his dream was not realized due to the prohibitive costs of mining and transporting the ore.

Some have suggested that his real concern was fur trading because his ship was meant to carry furs and trade items as well as ore, and his personal financial backers were fur merchants.

There was speculation that he used the ore project as a means to acquire his free lease on the fur trade, but I doubt that he would have been disappointed had he made a fortune from copper.

What's Happening at the Sault?

In 1731, the La Verendryes passed through the Sault on their trip to the west, but only found a few Indigenous people at the rapids and made no mention of any French there. Perhaps they did not stay long enough to meet the Sault's people, or they may have been here during the season when everyone was elsewhere.

There must have been Anishinaabe and French at the Sault because their religious records are at Michilimackinac which is where they went to be married or baptized.

Father Pierre Du Jaunay was at, what is now, Mackinaw City from 1735 to 1765. There is a record that states that he said mass at the Sault in 1741, and another record that shows that he travelled to the St. Joseph River (Niles, MI) which was a lengthy trip, for short visits in 1738, 1742, 1745 and 1752 to conduct religious ceremonies, but there was a French fort there to protect the Jesuits.

Perhaps, it was due to lack of protection for him that he did not visit the Sault more than once.

In any event, some of the names of people from the Sault who went to Michilimackinac for religious ceremonies during the eighteenth century were: Hamelin, La Gueniere, Sauvagesse, Chevalier, Parent, DuLignon, Rochereau, Cadot, Cadotte, Couvret, and Nolin, all noted as being voyageurs.

Throughout the eighteenth century, there was fur trade at the Sault and the French who lived here had Ojibway wives.

Records exist showing lengthy lists of men who were granted permits to the Sault each year for fur trading.

There were still canoes laden with furs passing along the St. Marys River from Lake Superior, headed for Québec.

France wanted to strengthen her defences wherever possible and that may have been why two French officers obtained a grant from the King, in 1750, to have a seigniory on the south side of the river at the Sault.

French Fort at the Sault

The location of the fort has been determined in detail. Arbic noted that "the fort site would apparently straddle Water Street, of today, about fifty feet east of Brady Street."

Fowle noted that during construction in 1908, was discovered "a fairly well-preserved stone and mortar foundation on the site of the old French fort as we have determined it. This was probably connected with the old fort as no other building is known to have occupied this spot."

Louis Legardeur de Repentigny was an officer in the French military, and Captain Louis de Bonne de Missègle, a nephew of the Marquis de la Jonquière, who was the governor of Canada at that time, was also an officer. They presented a petition to King Louis XV for a grant at the Sault covering land 18 miles (30 km) along the south side of the river by a depth from the river of 18 miles. The King signed his consent on June 24, 1751, to the grant with certain stipulations.

There was to be implementation of agriculture and the introduction of cattle. The idea of a fur trade was meant to be of much lesser importance. The fort was also meant to oppose expansion into the area by the English, to win over the Indigenous people, and be a place that provided safety and relaxation for the French who traded in the area as well as further north. It appears that De Bonne never came to the Sault.

By the time that De Repentigny got to the Sault, in 1751, there was only time to build a house before winter set in but this enabled him to entertain his fur trader neighbours who made a 90-mile snow-shoe trip from Mackinac to drop by for a visit

During winter, his hired men cut 1,100 pickets, each fifteen feet long, to create the palisade the following spring.

It cannot be determined where the hired men came from but perhaps they were fur traders who were wintering at the Sault.

The end result was a fort that enclosed four houses within a palisade that was 110 feet square.

One house was for the clerk. Another for the Interpreter, Cadotte, and his family. The two smallest houses were used as barracks for a small garrison.

As to farming, De Repentigny acquired a bull, two bullocks that were steers for beef, three cows, two heifers, one horse and a mare. It may have been a bit of a chore to transport these animals from Michilimackinac but it was done. The position of farmer was filled by hiring a Métis fur trader, residing at the Sault, named Jean Baptiste Cadotte, who began his farming experience by clearing the land and planting corn.

De Repentigny spent the winter of each year on his seigniory, while also pursuing the fur trade.

Then, early each spring, he canoed to Montreal with numerous voyageurs and Indigenous people to sell the furs that they had accumulated over the winter.

As already noted, the closest neighbours were at Michilimackinac, where there was a missionary, an army officer, and some French families.

It is certain there was travel back and forth between the Sault and Michilimackinac because there are religious records at Michilimackinac, setting out the details of the Cadotte's children.

When De Repentigny was called away to participate in the Seven Years' War, he found it too difficult to be at the Sault so that in January, 1757, he turned over his fur trade at the Sault, Michipicoten, and another area near Thunder Bay, to two traders, being De Langy and René de Couange, although De Repentigny was still to receive profits from the trade.

Meanwhile, in the east, hostility between the French and English for ownership of North America was brewing.

One of the battles involved the Englishman, Edward Braddock, with his 2,000 British regulars, who were soundly defeated in an ambush, by a French-Indigenous leader, born at Michilimackinac (now Mackinac City) named Charles-Michel Mouet de Langlade, who gave his name simply as Charles Langlade.

A troop of Indigenous people, as well as Métis, mainly from the area from Mackinac to the Sault, were commanded by Langlade in the battle that occurred near Fort Duquesne, now Pittsburgh, PA, in 1755.

Again, we see that the Saulteurs had not lost their fighting ability because they were credited with having played an important part in the battle.

Langlade fought extremely well in various battles throughout the war.

Seven years of war ended when the French surrendered Montreal to the English on September 8, 1759.

Now a lieutenant, Langlade returned to Mackinac, as commander, until September of 1761. As to the fate of the owners of the fort at the Sault, Captain de Bonne was killed during the war and De Repentigny eventually retired to France.

Old Woman Bay, Lake Superior, 2016

By Sheri Minardi Photography

The First Farmer

Jean Baptiste Cadotte was the son of Mathurin Cadeau who had attended the Pageant of St. Lusson in 1671.

William W. Warren, the noted Indigenous writer during the middle nineteenth century, wrote that Jean Baptiste Cadotte was Mathurin's son but, given Jean Baptiste Cadotte was born in 1723, I wonder if he might have been a grandson.

Warren stated that the name Cadeau was changed by the British to Cadotte. I think that he may have been the authority because Jean Baptiste Cadotte was his great-grandfather. That is, Jean Baptiste's son, Michel, had a daughter, named Mary, who married Warren's father, Lyman.

Cadotte first went to Lake Superior in 1742, travelling to out-of-the-way Ojibway villages, carrying items they wanted in exchange for their beaver furs.

Beginning in 1750, I would imagine that his farming activities were restricted to the summer and that he likely continued to pursue his trading business during spring and fall.

No records exist of any other tenant on the land except Cadotte but he did have the help of some Indigenous people with the work.

Cadotte became interested in a Saulteur girl named Anastasie Equawaice who was the daughter of Madjeckewiss, Chief of the A-waus-e clan, one of the principal divisions of the Ojibway.

Jean Baptiste and Anastasie were married on February 28, 1756, at Michilimackinac where, in due course, all of their children were baptized. There was a daughter born in 1756, another daughter in 1759, a son, also named Jean-Baptiste, in 1761, and a second son, Michel, in 1764. All of the Cadotte religious ceremonies were conducted by Father Pierre du Jaunay.

Mackinac Island had been an important place for the Anishinaabe.
Image courtesy of Native American Cultural History Trail as shown in www.spiritualtravels.info/

Alexander Henry

Alexander Henry was born in August of 1739, in New Jersey.

By age twenty, he was a merchant working out of Albany, N.Y. With three loaded batteaux, he travelled behind Major-General Jeffery Amherst along Lake Ontario to Montreal, providing supplies to the British army.

After Montreal surrendered in early September, 1760, Henry was told by a former fur trader, Jean Baptiste Leduc, about the business of trading at Michilimackinac and Lake Superior. Henry decided that this was for him so that during the spring of 1761, he became the second Englishman to acquire a fur-trade pass from Major-General Thomas Gage at Montreal.

Étienne Charles Campion was recommended to Henry as an assistant because Campion had become familiar with the upper Great Lakes region beginning in 1753 and by 1761 was an expert. With Campion as his guide, Henry organized a trading trip to Michilimackinac. The relationship worked so well that Campion stayed as Henry's assistant for the next two years.

When Henry arrived at La Cloche Island (near present day Little Current, Manitoulin Island) he went ashore and bartered for fish and dried meat. The Indigenous people were friendly toward him until they discovered that he was an Englishman. Then the trouble started. They told his men that the Indigenous people at Michilimackinac would kill him and pillage his cargo simply because he was English.

With that in mind, these Indigenous people decided that they may as well have a share of the take and demanded a keg of rum from him. Henry wrote that he "judged it prudent to comply." He did notice that the hostility was only against him. Regarding the French Canadians, their attitude was quite the opposite in that there was "most cordial good will."

Campion thought that it might help if Henry removed his English style clothes to give it a shot at trying to look like a Frenchman. Henry did what he could with what was available. He covered his middle with a cloth, put on a shirt – hanging loose, threw on a blanket coat, plopped a large red cap on his head, and finished off his new look by smearing his face and hands with dirt and grease.

Once they were on their way again, to get even more into the act, Henry took the place of one of his men in the canoe as a paddler. When Indigenous people approached, Henry used the paddle with as much skill as he possessed which, I gather, was not much at all. His lack of skill must not have been too noticeable because he did pass several Indigenous canoes without drawing attention to himself.

They arrived at Mackinac Island in the early part of September, 1761, where one of the Indigenous men took one look at him, laughed, and pointed him out to another, but that was the end of it.

As soon as he could, Henry left the island and headed across to the fort, which stood on the south side of the strait. He noted that the fort covered an area of two acres, contained thirty houses, and a church with a Jesuit missionary, with the entire area enclosed by tall cedar pickets.

Upon arrival at 4:00 p.m. at the fort, Henry transferred his trade wares to Campion as protection against pillage. At that point, they switched roles so that Campion was known as the trader. Although their voyageurs had been instructed not to let anyone know that Henry was English, the word got out.

The French Canadian militia, stationed at the fort, had their families with them. These family members had a business of outfitting canoes prior to their voyages either into the upper lakes or to Montreal. Some of them talked with Henry, and although they appeared friendly, they made it known to him that he should head for Detroit because, as an Englishman, he could not be safe at Michilimackinac.

It was Campion's opinion that the French inhabitants of the fort were more hostile toward the English than were the Indigenous people.

Henry quickly discovered that the Indigenous people were not about to accept an Englishman. To be on the safe side, Henry continued to try to look like a French trader but did not get far with this plan.

Before long, he received word that the entire band of Indigenous people from Mackinac Island had arrived with the intention of paying him a visit.

Minweweh, a war chief of the eastern section of the Ojibway, along with sixty of his warriors, entered the lodge where Henry was staying.

At first, they threatened Henry and it looked as if they were going to kill him, but then Minweweh gave a lengthy speech to Henry wherein he stated that the English King had done nothing for the Indigenous people, nor entered into any treaty with them. Therefore, the Indigenous people considered the French King to be their only friend. This gave them reason to continue to fight with the English. The Indigenous people had discussed Henry among themselves and their decision was that he had no plans to fight with them but was there to peacefully trade. For this reason, they advised him that they would consider him to be a brother.

Although Henry and Minweweh had become friends, Henry did not feel at ease until the British soldiers arrived to take over the post from Charles Langlade. Henry wrote, "Three Hundred troops, of the 60th Regiment, under the command of Lieutenant Leslie, marched into the fort; and this arrival dissipated all our fears . . ."

Henry sorted his goods, hired Canadian interpreters and clerks, and sent them out into Lakes Michigan and Superior. As a merchant, he remained at Michilimackinac for the winter although he was keen to visit the Sault.

On May 15, 1762, Henry left by canoe for the Sault, arriving on the nineteenth. He must have been quite affable because he appears to have had the ability to make friends quickly with everyone, including Jean Baptiste Cadotte and his family. No doubt, this ability was an asset to his business. Henry later described Cadotte's wife, Anastasie, as being "energetic," "hardy" and "fearless." He noted that she would travel great distances with a group of coureurs de bois in order to promote her husband's business interests among her many relatives.

Indigenous Gathering at Michilimackinac

About the Sault, Henry wrote: "The portage, or carrying-place, commences at the fort . . . Canoes, half loaded, ascend, on the south side, and the other half of the load is carried on men's shoulders."

He further noted that there were fifty warriors in the village and that the Indigenous people resided here during the summer but headed west in the winter to hunt. He indicated that the village "anciently" was much more populated.

I assume that he acquired this information from the locals.

Perhaps the constant warring among the Indigenous people caused many of them to relocate elsewhere. There was the possibility that many of them were in the area of Detroit at this time.

Henry's general comments about the Sault were that "During the summer, the weather was sometimes exceedingly hot. Pigeons were in great plenty; the stream supplied our drink; and sickness was unknown."

The combination of the "pleasant situation of the fort "and his desire to learn the Indigenous language made him decide to spend the next winter at the Sault.

The Cadotte family only spoke Chippewa so it was going to be an ideal environment for him to learn the language.

When the garrison of Royal Americans (60th Foot) led by Lieutenant John Jamet, arrived at the fort in the Sault in September, 1762, both Henry and Cadotte got along well with all of them.

Following Edward Braddock's defeat in 1755, this new regiment was meant to protect the frontier with some of them stationed at the Sault as a sub-post to the one at Michilimackinac.

Within the first two weeks of October, Henry had set himself and others up for the winter with the catch of about five hundred whitefish, each weighing from six to fifteen pounds. The fish were dried by hanging them, head down, on long horizontal poles, propped up with stakes, and then freezing them. How they managed to freeze them in October, I cannot imagine, but Henry wrote that this was the procedure, and that the fish stayed frozen until the following April.

Canoes filled with the excess fish were sent to Michilimackinac because Jamet did not think that his men would need to eat fish all winter. His thought was that, with the huge amount of liquor he had with him, wild game could be bought from the Indigenous people, but he was mistaken.

They were living quite happily in the fort with Cadotte until December 22, when, at 1:00 a.m., a fire broke out and raged through all of the houses except Cadotte's.

Jamet appeared to be trapped within the fire, but as Henry knew which room Jamet was sleeping in, he had the window of that room smashed, so that Jamet managed to escape but suffered severe injuries from the fire.

All of the regiment's provisions were completely burned, as well as a considerable amount of the fish.

Not a good end to 1762.

To save the soldiers from starvation, it was decided that they should move to Michilimackinac.

Just in the nick of time, the troops arrived there on the last day of December, being the day before ice set in which prevented movement by water until the following spring.

As Jamet was too injured to be moved at that time, he was taken in and cared for by the Cadotte family and Henry.

With their food supply destroyed, they hunted hares and partridges, and speared trout from the river.

It was not until February 20, 1763, that they considered it safe to walk on the frozen water.

With Jamet anxious to get to Michilimackinac, a group was assembled to take him there. The entourage included Cadotte, Henry, two French Canadians, and two Indigenous people.

The Canadians and Indigenous people transported the group's provisions of dry maize, fish, along with some pork and a few loaves of bread all of which were partly burned, on an Indigenous sled.

The trip by snowshoes was not easy, given the deep snow, and was a difficult method of travel for the inexperienced. Overall, the trip was slow and almost disastrous.

It was not until March 7th that they reached the half way mark. On this day, they discovered that the lake was still open, ice was drifting, and their food supply was nearly depleted.

There was no alternative but to send those who were experienced snowshoe travellers, being the Canadians and Indigenous people, back to the Sault for more food, or face starvation.

The food was safely obtained and the group started on again; however, now Jamet's feet were so blistered from the snowshoe cords that he could barely walk. Over the next three days, the group covered only a short distance.

Again, their food was running out so it was decided that Henry and one of the Canadians would proceed on to Michilimackinac to get help.

The next day, they arrived at the fort and arranged for a party to leave the following day to take food back to the others.

Three days later, Jamet safely arrived at the fort.

Cadotte made the return trip to the Sault but it is not known if anyone accompanied him.

Henry decided to stay at Michilimackinac for a short while, later returning to the Sault via the Bay of Boutchitaouy, now noted on maps as Saint Martin Bay, and then through the forest, arriving back at the Sault within two days.

Along the way, Henry suffered from snowshoe evil which is caused by a strain on the leg tendons due to the weight of the snowshoes, resulting in inflammation.

Soon after his arrival, he left the Sault again with the other residents to go to the maple sugar bush that was about three miles away, where they stayed until April 25th. This might have been Sugar Island.

During their first day back at the Sault, they were visited by Sir Robert Davers who was on a "voyage of curiosity."

Davers and Henry travelled together to Michilimackinac where Henry planned on staying until his clerks returned with the furs they had acquired over the winter. Once this business had been conducted, his plan was to return to the "Sault de Sainte-Marie."

When he reached Michilimackinac, other traders who had arrived, advised him that the Indigenous were planning an attack against the English. One trader, Laurent Ducharme, distinctly advised Major George Etherington about an imminent attack which would annihilate every Englishman in the area. The major chose to ignore the warning.

When Henry had first arrived at Michilimackinac back in 1761, he and Wawatam, a minor Ojibway chief, who was about age forty-five at the time, had become friends to the extent that Wawatam had welcomed Henry into his family as his brother.

On June 2, 1763, Wawatam paid Henry a visit and, without being free to explain his reasoning, tried to convince Henry to go to the Sault with him the next morning.

Henry's response was that he could not leave that soon but would go after his clerks returned.

Early the next morning, Wawatam, and his family, again asked him to leave for the Sault. Although Henry was now able to communicate in the Native's language, he did not recognize the nuances of danger in Wawatam's manner of speaking.

The following day, June 4th, was the English King's birthday which date became the focus of a surprise Indigenous attack, preplanned by Pontiac, against all Englishmen within the fort.

The Indigenous did not suddenly attack but created a friendly atmosphere wherein a game of lacrosse was arranged with much anticipation and advertisement.

Natives staging a deadly game of baggataway at Fort Michilimackinac in 1763
http://musquetry.blogspot.ca/2015/06

The attack had been organized by Minweweh, an Ojibway war chief on Mackinac Island, with the help of Madjeckewiss, Anastasie Cadotte's father. Madjeckewiss originated from the Sault; however, due to Cadotte's influence, the other Indigenous residing at the Sault did not take part in the attack.

Warren wrote that Cadotte convinced the majority of Ojibway that it was useless to fight the English because so many of their warriors would be killed in the process. Warren further maintained that it was Cadotte's influence that kept the Lake Superior Ojibways from joining Pontiac's war with the result that the Ojibways were not wiped out. This meant that during the mid-nineteenth century, they had a larger population than other Algonquins and were the largest tribe east of the Mississippi River.

On the day of the planned attack, an Indigenous fellow told Henry that a lacrosse game was about to start and asked him to come and watch it.

Henry did not have a good feeling after talking with the Indigenous fellow so went to talk with Major Etherington, suggesting that the Indigenous people might be up to no good. The commander paid no attention to him.

Henry did not go out to watch the game.

A canoe was leaving for Montreal the following day and Henry wanted to send letters with it. While he was writing, he suddenly heard the Indigenous war cry.

In the midst of the game, the attack began. He looked out a window and saw the English being savagely killed and in particular, witnessed the death of Jamet.

Henry grabbed a gun but then realized that he was not going to win against four hundred Indigenous. He then noticed that the French were doing nothing and were not being attacked. This gave him the idea to hide in one of their houses.

It was Charles Langlade's house, next door, where he ran for cover. When he asked to be hid in a safe place within his house, Langlade basically asked what Henry wanted him to do, suggesting that he could do nothing for him. However, a Pawnee woman, who was a slave belonging to Langlade, indicated for him to follow her. She hid him in the attic where, through a crack, Henry could see the Englishmen being killed by the Indigenous people.

Later, the Indigenous people came to Langlade's home searching for any Englishmen. Hearing them talk, Henry hid behind some large birch bark containers that were stored there to be used in making maple sugar. Four Indigenous people entered the attic to look around. Henry did not know how they missed seeing him, but they did. After they left, he thought perhaps any danger to him had passed, so he fell asleep on a feather bed that was sitting on the floor of the room. The following day, again some Indigenous people returned to Langlade's house, telling him that they had not found Henry among the dead so that their suspicion was that Langlade must know where he was. Langlade's wife, Charlotte-Ambroisine, was afraid that the Indigenous people might harm her children out of revenge if Henry was not turned over to them. Therefore, Langlade decided he had better disclose Henry's whereabouts. He let them know that he had discovered that Henry was hiding in his attic, without his permission. He then took the Indigenous people to the attic where, this time, Henry was in plain sight. At first it seemed that one of the Indigenous people named Wenniway, who actually knew Henry, was going to drive a large carving knife into Henry's chest. There was nothing Henry could do to stop the attack because Wenniway was six feet tall, or more. Wenniway grabbed Henry by his coat collar with one hand. The Indigenous guy looked into Henry's eyes for some anxious seconds, then Wenniway dropped his arm, while saying, "I won't kill you!" He then explained to Henry that he had killed many in battles against the English, but during one battle his own brother, Musinigon, had been killed. He then decided that Henry should be named after this deceased brother.

Initially, Wenniway planned on holding Henry prisoner in his cabin. Henry was terrified that some other Native, who perhaps was under the influence of alcohol, might kill him, so he pleaded that it would not be safe for him to be found in Wenniway's cabin. When Henry asked Langlade if he would keep him instead, Wenniway agreed to this plan until such time as he could safely take Henry away.

There were ninety troops at the fort, and out of that number, seventy of them were brutally killed. As it turned out, only one of the English traders, named Tracy, was murdered. Father du Jaunay managed to bring the vicious slaughter to an end. It is thought that he arranged to have the deceased British buried in the post's cemetery.

Langlade, who had told Etherington that he had heard that the Ojibway planned to attack, had been ignored.

Later, when Etherington and William Leslie, were both tied to stakes, shortly to be burned, Langlade put his own life in jeopardy to save their lives. It was then thanks to Langlade's Ottawa relatives that the other English traders, as well as the remaining soldiers, were protected from further attacks, and in due course, were taken to Montreal.

Unbeknown to Henry at that time was that Wawatam had obtained the promise from the Ojibway chief that Henry would not be harmed. Four days after the attack, while Henry was in the prison lodge with the chiefs, Wawatam arrived.

To secure Henry's release, both Wawatam and his wife carried in a load of merchandise which they gave to the chiefs. Wawatam took Henry to his own lodge where his entire family greeted him and prepared a meal for him, which was the first he had had since he was captured.

By now the local Indigenous people, made up of 350 men capable of fighting, did not think that they had enough strength to fight the English.

Therefore, on June 9th, an Indigenous council was held where it was decided to move to Mackinac Island for defence against a possible attack by the English. Several days after their arrival on the island, two large canoes arrived from Montreal. The property in the canoes belonged to a Mr. Levy but had the voyageurs told the Indigenous people that the goods were owned by a French Canadian, the goods would not have been touched by them. This was not the case; therefore, the Indigenous people seized everything. There was a considerable amount of liquor among the goods which the Indigenous people proceeded to zealously consume.

Wawatam wanted to join his friends in drinking the liquor but at the same time was concerned for Henry's safety. He took Henry to the high land in the middle of the island, instructing him to hide there until he returned for him. It was after Henry had slept there for two nights when Wawatam returned for him.

A few days later, Menehwehna, a great chief of the village of Michilimackinac, came to Wawatam's lodge to advise that Indigenous people were arriving from Detroit. His concern was that because some of the Indigenous people had friends and relatives who had been killed by the English that they would retaliate against any Englishman they happened to meet. He advised that Henry should be given a major makeover so that he would look Native.

By now, Henry was well accustomed to changing his looks, so he readily agreed. Menehwehna, along with Wawatam and his family, put the plan into motion immediately by cutting Henry's hair, shaving his head, except for a narrow strip on the top, and painting his face with three or four colours which included red and black. One of them painted a shirt red. Then, a collar of wampum was put around his neck with another one attached to his chest. Bands of silver were put on Henry's upper arms, with smaller bands on his wrists. Hose, made of scarlet cloth were put on his legs. Over his shirt and hose was added a scarlet blanket. To top him off, a bunch of feathers were somehow placed on his head. His makeover complete, the Indigenous people thought that Henry now looked quite handsome.

Soon there was a lack of food so they left the island and proceeded to the Bay of Boutchitaouy, about twelve miles away, where they found plenty of wildfowl and fish.

While in the bay, Wawatam's daughter-in-law went into labour with her first child. She was put into a small lodge constructed for her own use during labour, which was built by the woman in half an hour. By the next morning she was very ill, although Henry wrote that cases of difficult labour are very rare among Indigenous women. Wawatam asked Henry to go with him to locate a snake, which he did. The blood from the snake was mixed with water and given to the girl. Within one hour, a healthy child was delivered. Wawatam declared that the remedy never failed! The very next day, the new mother assisted in loading the canoe.

Henry found the Indigenous peoples' medical information regarding disease and remedies interesting. He wrote that in general, the

Indigenous people did not suffer from diseases other than illnesses relating to lung inflammations, and rheumatism among the elderly. He attributed lung ailments to the constant exposure to wet and cold weather, sleeping on the ground, and breathing night air.

With regard to flesh wounds, he noted that the Indigenous people certainly had "astonishing cures." At the Sault, he knew a man who was struck with an axe in his side, during a quarrel, and the axe was so deep that it could not be easily removed. Before attempting to deal with the axe, the doctor gave the injured man a white substance mixed with water to swallow which caused the man to throw up a blood clot. The doctor then proceeded to deal with the wound by cutting away more of it. The man was walking within six days. Twenty years later he was still alive.

Henry continued to live and travel with Wawatam and his family for hunting and fishing until the following spring when he returned to Michilimackinac, where the only traders he found were two Frenchmen.

Eight days after arriving at Michilimackinac, a group of Indigenous people from Saginaw arrived. They advised him that as he was the only Englishman there, they were going to kill him. With that, Henry asked Wawatam to take him to the Sault where he knew the Indigenous people were peaceful and he could count on his friend, Cadotte, to keep him safe.

Wawatam and his family left with Henry during the night. On the way to the Sault, at Isle aux Outardes, Wawatam's wife, Nonen, became ill so they had to stop.

While there, a canoe approached that Henry determined carried Canadians, based on the way they paddled, as well as by their skin tone. He thought it was a canoe heading for Montreal, but then discovered that three Canadians were taking Anastasie Cadotte from Michilimackinac to the Sault. After greetings were exchanged, Mrs. Cadotte happily agreed that Henry could join them. He then removed his Indigenous dress and put on a Canadian blanket coat and tied a handkerchief around his head. Henry wrote that the reason for the handkerchief was because hats were not often worn in this area.

It was a good thing that he did change because on the second morning of their trip, they noticed a fleet of twenty canoes behind them, who managed to catch-up with them.

When the canoes had surrounded them, one of the Indigenous people mentioned that he suspected that Henry was an Englishman. Henry pretended that he could not understand them while Anastasie assured them that he was a French Canadian, on his first voyage from Montreal. The next day, they arrived at the Sault, safe and sound, where Henry received a "generous welcome" from his friend, Cadotte.

It was now May of 1764. Thirty warriors were at the Sault but they did not plan on joining the Indigenous war against the English due to Cadotte's persuasion to stay out of it.

Henry wrote that for the next five days his life was "tranquil" but on the sixth day a young

Indigenous fellow advised Cadotte that some warriors had arrived from Michilimackinac and were looking for Henry with intentions that were less than friendly.

At almost the same time, a message came from the chief of the village, advising Henry to hide himself until it could be determined what the visitors were up to. Once again, Henry hid in an attic. Soon after, the Indigenous people, led by Madjeckewiss, arrived at Cadotte's home. Madjeckewiss acknowledged their intent to harm Henry but also advised that they wanted to raise a party of warriors to go with them to Detroit.

Cadotte immediately called together all the chiefs and warriors of the village, as well as the recently arrived warriors, and then both Cadotte and the village chief gave speeches to those assembled, making it clear that they were protecting Henry, and that none of the village warriors would go to Detroit with Madjeckewiss.

Right after the speeches, they were told that a canoe had just arrived from Niagara. This was a place from which everyone was anxious to hear news. A message was sent for everyone, including the visitors, to attend a council. At the council the newly arrived advised that they had been sent by Sir William Johnson to advise all Indigenous people to come to Fort Niagara to arrange peace with the English. The alternative was that they would be destroyed by the English before fall arrived.

The matter was discussed and it was decided that sixteen men would be sent to Niagara to meet with Sir William Johnson. Henry was one of those who wanted to attend because it would give him a chance to get out of the upper country (pays d'en haut) to which request and reasoning, the village chief was in agreement. They immediately left for Niagara

When the group passed La Cloche, they noticed that many of its inhabitants were not there and concluded that they had already gone to meet with Johnson.

Upon reaching Fort Niagara, Henry met Colonel John Bradstreet who informed him that he was going to Detroit and from there would be sending troops to Michilimackinac. He assured Henry that he could safely return to Michilimackinac with the regiment to recover his assets there. Henry was made a commander of a corps, although he stated, "of which, I can give no very flattering account."

At Detroit, the Indigenous people present agreed to peace terms. The agreement is known as the 1764 Treaty of Niagara. Stemming from this treaty was the agreement by the Indigenous people that they would defend the English Crown in future conflicts. That they have done, and at present represents 247 years of defence, both at home within Canada and abroad on behalf of Canada.

The next day, Captain William Howard, with two companies, three hundred Canadian volunteers, and Henry, left for Fort Michilimackinac, arriving there on September 22nd. Troops were not sent to the Sault because Howard planned on relying upon Cadotte to represent him there.

Upon arriving at Michilimackinac, the Ottawas of L'Arbre Croche (now Harbor Springs, MI) were notified to attend at the fort, which summons they obeyed, bringing with them some Chippewa chiefs. After discussion, peace was concluded with both.

Henry proceeded on to the Sault to collect his property, which I gather must have been furs that had been left there for him after he had departed for Niagara. Once he arrived at the Sault, he decided to spend the winter there with his friends. He would go back to Michilimackinac the following spring.

In May, 1765, Cadotte told the Indigenous people about the negotiations for peace undertaken by Sir William Johnson, and one month later, he led eighty canoes to Michilimackinac for the purpose of creating a treaty. As part of the negotiations, the Indigenous people asked that traders be allowed to go to Lake Superior because this would save them having to travel to Montreal to trade their furs for items they wanted or needed.

Johnson granted the exclusive trade of Lake Superior to Henry who immediately purchased goods from the post at Michilimackinac, on twelve months' credit. His supply of goods, that filled four canoes, was calculated at the "price of ten thousand pounds weight of good and merchantable beaver," which was Michilimackinac currency. He hired twelve men, at 250 livres each, or a hundred pounds of beaver skins, to transport his merchandise to his wintering location on Lake Superior. In addition, Henry bought fifty bushels of maize, one of which was the equivalent of ten pounds of beaver skins.

On July 14, 1765, Henry left for the Sault where he took Cadotte as a partner in his trading business, although their agreement specified that Cadotte would stay at the Sault.

After a short visit, of slightly less than two weeks, Henry headed out to his wintering place in Chequamegon Bay. Upon his arrival there, he advanced necessities required by the Indigenous people, after which they left to travel a distance of three hundred miles to hunt. Henry was provided with "a very comfortable house" at Chequamegon where his main winter pastime was spearing trout through holes cut in the lake's ice.

In mid-May, 1766, the Indigenous people returned with fifteen thousand pounds of beaver furs, as well as otter and marten skins. Henry then disposed of his remaining merchandise and headed toward Michilimackinac, accompanied by fifty canoes of Indigenous people, who still had one hundred packs of beaver, which Henry had been unable to purchase from them.

On his way to Michilimackinac, Henry took a side trip, with Indigenous guides, ten miles up the Ontonagon River to see a mass of copper that weighed, according to his estimate, at least five tons. He wrote that it was pure copper, and that with an axe, he had cut off a piece of it, weighing one hundred pounds.

Henry spent the winter of 1766-1767 at the Sault where there was an early frost and, for some quirk of nature, there was a lack of fish. He sent five men some distance to another post, but they returned the day before Christmas without food of any sort. Henry had heard that fish might be found in Oak-bay, now known as Goulais Bay on the north side of the St. Marys River. He took several men, with a pint of maize for each, and off they went.

After being at Goulais Bay for two weeks, the fish swam elsewhere. The men then returned to the Sault hoping that by then some fish had arrived there, but none had. A decision was made to head for Michilimackinac, taking with them only one meal for each person. Their luck changed at their first encampment, where within one hour, they caught seven trout, each of which weighed from ten to twenty pounds. As they proceeded on, they met a group of Indigenous people who had plenty of fish and generously shared their fish with them. The next day, as they continued on, a caribou was spotted, which Henry killed. The carcass weighed about four hundred pounds, providing the group with enough food for two days.

On the seventh day of their trip, they arrived at Michilimackinac about which Henry wrote "our difficulties ended." He remained there during the summer because on July 1, 1767, he wrote that one hundred canoes arrived from the northwest, loaded with beaver furs.

Working for Robert Rogers, commandant at Michilimackinac, and also for Johnson, Cadotte had become one the most influential people in the Upper Lakes.

In March, 1767, Cadotte persuaded the Indigenous people at the Sault to exchange their French flag for a British one. During the summer, Cadotte joined Henry Bostwich, John Chinn, and

Alexander Henry in the search for copper deposits along Lake Superior. Cadotte, as an associate of Bostwich, maintained good relations with the Indigenous people, keeping them from interfering with the mining sites. Regrettably, the operation was not profitable.

For the winter of 1767-1768, Henry decided that his wintering ground would be at Michipicoten. On reaching the old French trading post, which perhaps was built by De Repentigny, Henry found Indigenous people inhabiting ten lodges. This was perfect for his business. Goods required by the Indigenous people were distributed to them and credit was extended to each man for the collection of one hundred beaver skins and thirty skins by each woman. Henry's impression of them was that they were honest people, of good character, so he felt that there would be no problem extending credit to them.

Henry remained at the post during the winter, noting that the lake was frozen over by Christmas, and passing the time by hunting hares, partridges, and the odd caribou.

When not hunting, he enjoyed cooking the food he was able to easily obtain. He did not note who was with him, but there must have been people, whether Indigenous or French, cannot be determined. When he wrote about making maple sugar beginning in early April, he refers to "we" instead of "I."

In preparing to make maple sugar, he dug out the snow from a hollow where he built a house. Although the house was seven feet high, the snow around it was deeper than seven feet. Until May

12th, his time was consumed with making maple sugar. During this time, no other food was consumed. He wrote that each man ate a pound of maple sugar per day, had no desire for anything else, and actually felt satisfied.

When Henry returned to the river banks he noticed that birds had appeared to such an extent that enough could be shot in one day to feed fifty men. It was less than a week when the birds left the area, flying to the north.

Once the maple sugaring was completed, the Indigenous people started to arrive with the two thousand beaver furs they had gathered during the winter. Some of them told him that they had been to a Hudson's Bay factory.

There was a small loss, which Henry considered "trivial" which happened because one of the Indigenous people had died during the hunt. The deceased's relatives wanted to pay the balance owed because they believed that his soul would not be peaceful as long as he had a debt.

Sugar Making in Canada (1849) painting by
Cornelius Krieghoff

In the spring of 1768, Henry returned to
Michilimackinac, where he met Alexander Baxter,
who had travelled from England, to investigate
ores in the area. Henry discussed the ore
possibilities with Baxter, describing the specimen
he had obtained, and relating his observations. As a
result of this meeting, Henry entered into a
partnership agreement with Baxter to mine silver
around Lake Superior.

In the meantime, Henry again decided to
spend the winter of 1768-1769 at Michipicoten,
given he had had such an enjoyable, as well as
successful, experience there the previous winter. It
was during October when he arrived at
Michipicoten. Immediately, he disbursed
merchandise to the Indigenous people, who then
set out on their winter hunt.

At that point, he decided to treat himself to a visit to the Sault. Along with him went three Canadians and a young Indigenous woman who wanted to visit her relatives there. As the trip was thought to be short, they planned on fishing along the way, so that the only food that they took with them was one quart of maize per person.

Once the sun went down on their first day, they settled on an island, setting their fishing net for the night. During the night a violent storm began that continued for the next three days. Given they could not get to their fishing net, they ate the maize. There was some concern when they discovered that the storm had swept away their net but they continued on their way to the Sault. Again, they settled on an island for the night. That evening, and for the next nine days, gale force winds prevented them from putting their canoe into the lake.

Henry went hunting on the island but found nothing. By the third day, he was almost too weak to walk and had to take frequent breaks to be able to keep going. He did manage to get two snowbirds. When he returned to their camp from hunting, one of the Canadians told him that the other two Canadians had proposed to kill and eat the young woman.

When Henry questioned them about this, they readily admitted that they thought it would be their only way to survive. One of them explained to him that he had previously had an experience, while wintering in the northwest, when he had survived by eating human flesh. This was not the answer that Henry was hoping for. The next morning, he climbed a mountain where he found lichen growing on the rocks. He already knew that lichen could take the place of food when famine was threatened. When he consulted the young woman, she told him that lichen could be made edible by boiling it down. Before long, they had a satisfying meal. Who would have thought that lichen could be a lifesaver!

The wind died down on the ninth evening. Although everyone was weak, they were anxious to get on their way. The next morning, they had a streak of luck when they met two canoes of Indigenous people, on their way from the Sault, who had plenty of fish which they shared with them. Upon receiving the fish, they beached their canoe, lit a fire, and had a plentiful fish fry. By that same night, they reached the Sault, where they stayed to visit for a few days. I doubt that I ever would have left again, but I am not as hardy, or as brave, as they were. In the spring of 1769, as soon as the ice on the lake had melted, Henry, along with two Indigenous people, canoed to Michipicoten Island, which Henry found to be one solid rock. He was discouraged when he found that it contained nothing valuable; however, the Indigenous people told him about another nearby island that they described as being covered with yellow sand. They explained that on a clear day that island could be seen from Michipicoten Island. They waited for the haze covering the area to clear, but after two days, it still had not lifted. Disheartened, Henry returned to his post.

In 1770, Alexander Baxter returned with legal papers whereby he and Henry entered into a formal agreement for working the mines of Lake Superior. Henry wrote that the two of them spent the winter at the Sault building a barge as well as laying the keel of a forty-ton sloop.

The shipyard was at Point aux Pins, on the north side of the St. Marys River, due to its safe harbour. Benjamin Frobisher, in a letter written in 1784, stated that Baxter also lived there.

In early in May, 1771, when the ice had cleared from the lake, they left Point aux Pins and set sail for the island where they expected to find yellow sand that was going to make their fortunes. They spent two days just searching for the island but when they landed on it, there was disappointment. They did stay for three days but did not find yellow sand or gold. While there, Henry shot some caribous that he decided must have got onto the island via drifting ice. Otherwise, he noticed an abundance of Hawks that circled around them to the extent that they had to watch out for their noses. Henry wrote, "One of them actually took my cap from off my head." That island is now known as Caribou Island which is in Lake Superior, due west of Agawa Bay, Ontario.

On the fourth day of their trip, they left for Nanibojou, which is at the northwest of Lake Superior, near Grand Marais, Minnesota They reached it within eighteen hours due to a good wind. The next day, the coast was examined where several veins of copper and lead were located, following which, they returned home.

Once at Point aux Pins they began constructing an air-furnace. Meanwhile, the ores collected by them, on their trip, were examined. Their assayer reported that the lead ore contained silver in the proportion of forty ounces to a ton but the copper ore was not ideal.

They then decided to venture over to Iroquois Point, across the bay, to have a look at what might be contained in the stones there, but there was no report made so perhaps nothing notable was sighted.

Next, they headed west to Ontonagon, where they built a house, while sending back to the Sault for provisions. Upon digging, their miners discovered copper, some of which weighed three pounds. Once everything was arranged for the miners to stay the winter, Henry and Baxter again returned to the Sault.

John Johnston, of the Sault, in 1809 wrote that some of the work by the miners was done at what is now Miner's Bay, an inlet in Alger County, Michigan, and quite a distance east of Ontonagon.

Early in the spring of 1772, Henry and Baxter sent a boatload of provisions to the miners.

To their surprise, on June 20th, it came back accompanied by all the miners who reported that it would take much more labour and considerable expense to continue mining the area.

It was concluded that it would be too difficult to provide food for the number of men that would be required to mine the area.

Henry and Baxter launched their sloop, in August, which carried miners to a vein of copper on the north side of Lake Superior.

Little was accomplished during the winter but between the spring and fall of 1773, they penetrated 30 feet into the solid rock, although the rock was blasted with great difficulty. At the beginning, the vein was four feet wide but diminished to four inches. Therefore, they stopped the work and transported the miners back to the Sault.

Then the disheartening communication arrived that their English investors would not advance funds for future expenses. Therefore, in 1774, Baxter disposed of the sloop and other assets, paid the outstanding debts of the enterprise, and called it a day. Another reason for halting the expedition was due to the prohibitive cost of transporting the metal to Montreal. This expense would exceed market value of the metal. The aim of the company had really been to mine silver but this was not to be.

Meanwhile, Henry had continued in the fur trade. In 1775, Henry, Cadotte, Peter Pond, Joseph and Thomas Frobisher, along with a large group of other traders, travelled west and traded in a lucrative joint venture, and because of this, the Sault became important as a provisioning post.

In the fall of 1777, Henry sold his business at Michipicoten to Jean-Baptiste Nolin and Venance Lemaire, *dit* Saint-Germain. The following year, Henry traded at the Sault, working with Cadotte, but in partnership with John Chinn. It is believed that this was Henry's last year in the Sault.

Thereafter, Henry moved to Montreal, although he stayed in the fur trade for some time. On June 11, 1785, at age forty-five years, he married a widow, Julia Ketson, with whom he had a daughter and four sons.

Henry again traded at Michilimackinac from 1785 to 1790. During the mid-1780s, he developed a plan to market furs in China and passed along his ideas to John Jacob Astor. Then, in the 1790s, Henry and Astor assisted the North West Company in organizing shipments of furs to China. In 1792, Henry had a share in the North West Company but in 1796 he sold his interest, although he continued to buy furs from traders and export them to England.

In 1809, in New York, he published his memoirs of the years 1760 to 1776. Without the publication of Henry's memoirs, we would not have the amazing details regarding life in our area during that period.

After an adventurous and respected life, Alexander Henry died at Montreal, at age 84 years.

Agawa Bay on Lake Superior

By Sheri Minardi Photography

Jean Baptiste Nolin

Nolin and his partner purchased the trading post at Michipicoten from Alexander Henry for the price of fifteen thousand livres. They then hired a few men to work there for them. The American Revolution created problems for the business in that goods shipped from Montreal to be traded at the post were not getting through to the post. As a result, the business was not as successful as had been anticipated. Nolin quit trading at Michipicoten by 1781 and went to Mackinac Island. He spent some years going back and forth between Mackinac Island and the Sault but put down permanent roots in the Sault.

Nolin married Marie-Angélique Couvret. Her father was voyageur, Joseph-Victor Couvret, and her mother was Marie-Charlotte, an Ojibway of the Sault, who had been married at Michilimackinac on October 13, 1749. Over the ensuing years, at least some of the Nolin children were sent to Montreal to become well educated.

Persuaded by his mother-in-law, Marie-Charlotte, Nolin bought a large piece of land at the Sault, in 1794, behind the fort occupied by Cadotte and his family. Finally, Cadotte had permanent neighbours who were closer than Mackinac Island. At some point, Nolin acquired property on the north side of the river which eventually was sold to Charles Oakes Ermatinger. In due course, Nolin developed an opulent lifestyle.

Nolin was the agent at the Sault for the North West Company. As the agent, he was the middleman for trade goods shipped from Montreal to be paid to the Indigenous people in exchange for the furs they had trapped during the winter. In addition, he arranged for white fish to be salted and then supplied to the local voyageurs, as well as shipped to Mackinac Island and Detroit. By 1806, the Michilimackinac Company began providing trade goods to Nolin, instead of the North West Company. It would appear that Nolin then became associated with the Michilimackinac Company as its agent. Eventually, in 1819, Nolin sold his interests in the Sault to Ermatinger because he had been encouraged by Lord Selkirk, who also provided incentives, to move west. The Nolin family then established new roots in Pembina, North Dakota.

Theresa Schenck wrote in *Who Owns Sault Ste. Marie* that Nolin settled in the Sault, on the south side of the river, in 1788, and at that time there were seven houses there occupied by ten fur traders, with the names Jean Baptiste Cadotte, Joseph DuChene, Jean Baptiste LaChausse, Pierre Parrent, Jean Baptiste Lurrent, and Lavoine Barthe, Françoise Cameraire, Joseph Piquette and his son Françoise, Jean Baptiste Perrault, and John Sayer who was an Irish merchant.

Cadotte's Elder Years

About 1767, following the death of his wife, Anastasie, Cadotte married a French Canadian named Marie Mouet, who presented him with a son, Joseph-Marie, in October of that year. As well, there is a baptism record, dated July 28, 1768, for their daughter, named Marie.

Between the years 1773-1780, Cadotte's son, Jean Baptiste, attended the College Saint Raphael, in Montreal. It is possible that Cadotte's other children also were educated in Montreal because it was common for fur traders of some wealth to send their children there to obtain a good education.

In 1780, it can be said that Cadotte played a part in the American Revolution. He was asked by the Lieutenant Governor of Michilimackinac, Patrick Sinclair, to enlist the help of the Indigenous people, living along the southern shore of Lake Superior, to join a force that would attack the Spanish in St. Louis, Missouri. Sinclair stated, "the Indians are under the absolute authority of Mr. Cadotte, who is a very honest man." There were Indigenous people who did help in the attack; however, it was not successful.

In September, 1783, Daniel Robertson, commandant at Michilimackinac, sent Cadotte, as government interpreter, along with Madjeckewiss, to the Chequamegon region in an unsuccessful effort to stop a war between the Ojibway and the Foxes and Sioux.

This was an about-face for Madjeckewiss, who last we heard of, was threatening to kill any Englishman he could find. Now he appeared to be trying to help an Englishman.

By 1786, both of Cadotte's sons, Jean Baptiste and Michel, were working with him under the name of Messrs. Cadotte and Company, and although beginning in the following year the sons fully carried out the operations of the business, it was not until May 24, 1796 that Cadotte, Sr. formerly turned over the company to his two sons. By this time, Cadotte, Sr. was extremely weak due to failing health.

During his career, Cadotte had been the major trader at the Sault, and although he never became wealthy, mainly because of his generosity to others, he did appear to have had a very comfortable income.

Cadotte remained on the seigniory for about fifty years and over those years, he went from being French, to English, and finally to American.

Incidentally, Louis-Honoré Fréchette published a collection of poems entitled La légende d'un peuple in Paris, in 1887. One of his poems was Le drapeau Fantôme, of which Cadotte was the main character.

Some references stated that his death was in about 1800, but Fréchette wrote that it was in

1818. I am not aware of his burial site, presumably in Sault, Michigan, but I find it disappointing that there is no designation.

Cadotte's two sons, Jean Baptiste Cadotte, Jr. and Michel Cadotte, also became traders among the Ojibway, and both men married Ojibway women.

Michel married the daughter of White Crane, hereditary chief of La Pointe village. Their daughter, Mary, was married to Lyman Warren, in 1821, at Mackinac.

Eventually, Michel died at La Pointe in 1836 at 72 years.

John Johnston

Johnston had been born in 1762 into a wealthy family of Antrim County in Northern Ireland, near Belfast. By 1790, he was in Montreal, and in 1791, he was on his way to Michilimackinac, arriving there on May 16, nearly devoured by mosquitos. He went on to winter at LaPointe where in due course he learned the Ojibway language and customs. While there he asked the chief if he could have permission to marry his daughter, Oshaguscodawaqua. The chief advised that he would have to marry her for life but first he had to wait one year to show that his intentions were honourable. Following this conversation, Johnston travelled to Montreal with his furs, returning to LaPointe during the summer of 1792, at which time he married her according to Ojibway custom.

It is believed that John Johnston set up a residence on the south side of the river at the Sault in 1793, close to that of Jean-Baptiste Cadotte.

Johnston did well as an independent fur trader among the Ojibway and, in this regard, his wife would have been an invaluable asset. Sometime later, he married his wife again on St. Joseph Island and at this time gave her the name of Susan. He never gave any thought to returning to Northern Ireland to live because he did not feel that Susan would be happy there. It would have been quite a jolt to her to join such a drastically different culture.

Later, in 1809, Johnston took his nine-year-old daughter, Jane, with him to Cork, Dublin, and

Wexford, Ireland, where he dealt with his inheritance, and then went to London to conduct other business, returning to Montreal in November of 1810.

Johnston decided he wanted to give up fur trading, move his family near to Montreal, and start a small farm. Before he blinked, the war of 1812 was on. He lived on American soil but was "true blue" to Britain which ultimately caused serious financial problems for him.

North West Company

Until the Jay Treaty, which became effective in mid-1796, the North West Company had a trading post on the south side of the St. Marys River. It was then obliged to vacate American soil. At that time, the Ojibway owned all of the land on the north side of the river; however, the Company obtained permission from the Ojibway to set up its business there, close to the foot of the rapids, where it built storage buildings and at least one residence. A sawmill was constructed in 1797.

Between the years 1797 and 1798, a canoe lock, with a nine-foot lift, for canoes and batteaux was built to avoid having to portage around the rapids. There is a replica of this canoe lock at 75 Huron Street, near the former St. Marys Paper Inc. building, which I understand was built on top of the original canoe lock. The blockhouse that was constructed is now situated at the Ermatinger Old Stone House on Queen Street East.

About 1791, John Sayer became an agent for the North West Company in the Sault, although it does not appear that he was often at the Sault. He entered into ongoing one-year trading contracts with Jean-Baptiste Perrault and Jean-Baptiste Cadotte, of the Sault. It appears that Sayer became a North West partner in 1798 and retired in 1807. He produced three children with his Indigenous wife, Obemau-unoqua (Nancy): Pierre-Guillaume, John Charles, and Henry, all of whom were later abandoned by Sayer.

Indigenous Women and the Fur Trade

Sylvia Van Kirk, in her book entitled *Many Tender Ties Women in Fur-Trade Society, 1670 – 1870,* describes the many ways that Indigenous women were imperative to the fur trade.

It was common practice for the men of the fur trade to take Indigenous wives à la façon du pays which is to say that the marriage was not conducted by a clergyman, not that there were clergymen available anyway.

Women played a very important role in ensuring that the fur trade operated well and smoothly.

Their responsibilities included assisting in the making of canoes by gathering roots from spruce trees, to be split to use as seams, and collecting spruce gum to caulk the seams. They made a vast number of moccasins from moose skin, given that a pair only lasted about one day.

They prepared the sinews and webbing of showshoes, without which men could not step outside in winter.

The women took responsibility to gather and chop wood.

Where it was a staple, and taken by canoe brigades on their trips, the women prepared the pemmican and created bags from skins to carry it.

As to fishing, in the fall, the women split and dried fish for winter.

Where rice was a staple, the women harvested it.

Making maple sugar, which was considered to be very valuable, was another task.

It was their job to also gather berries of whatever type was available.

They displayed much ability in snaring partridges and hares, often being away from home for a few weeks at a time to do so.

Their knowledge of Indigenous culture and language was the ultimate assistance to the traders.

They acted as guides, interpreters, and managed cultural differences between the Indigenous people and the traders.

Nineteenth Century

Charles Oakes Ermatinger and Mananowe Katawabidai

Charles Oakes Ermatinger was born in Montreal in 1776, to an English mother and a father of Swiss-German descent, who had emigrated to Montreal in 1760. At age nineteen, Ermatinger began his life in the fur trade, in 1795, as a clerk for the North West Company.

In 1799, the North West Company sent Ermatinger to Sandy Lake, which was due west of present-day Duluth, Minnesota, to spend the winter. During that winter, he took a wife in the Ojibway style of marriage, being Mananowe (Pleasing Voice) Katawabidai, later referred to as Charlotte Kattoonaluté. Mananowe was the daughter of Ojibway Chief Katawabidai and his father was Chief Bi-aus-wah who, legend says, lived to be 109 years old.

There was no formal civil or religious marriage ceremony. The procedure, prior to co-habiting with each other, was to gain her father's approval, and perhaps to give him a gift. It is not known if any rituals existed to signify the marriage. After more than thirty-two years of co-habitation, Charles and

Charlotte were married in Christ Church, in Montreal, on September 6, 1832, which was one year prior to his death.

It was common for fur traders to take a country wife, later abandon her and their children, return to Lower Canada (Quebec) and marry a non-Indigenous woman in a religious ceremony.

At some point, Ermatinger wrote to advise his nephew, who was a clerk with the Hudson's Bay Company, to avoid relationships with the Indigenous people, and not to enter into a country marriage, so as to allow him to remain independent and be free to leave Upper Canada when it suited him, without regrets. Given Ermatinger always stayed with his Indigenous country wife, and more than thirty years later, married her in church, makes me wonder why he gave this advice to his nephew. By all accounts, he had been a loving and dedicated husband and father.

My own ancestors did not abandon their Indigenous wives and children and did not return, in due course, to Lower Canada to reside. My great-great-great grandparents signed a marriage contract on July 28, 1825, and the groom posted a $500 bond which meant that if he left his wife, she had the financial security of the bond. I believe he paid the money to his bride's brother. The trousseau came from France. French relatives from Montreal attended the lavish wedding celebration on Drummond Island on August 3, 1828. William Solomon, a justice of the peace and grandfather of the bride, was one of the witnesses to the marriage vows. Following the wedding, the couple travelled to the Sault, by canoe, for their honeymoon. The first ceremony was considered to be legal; however, later, a Methodist minister came through the area and performed a religious service. Still later, they were married a third time by a Catholic priest. This may have been when they travelled to Penetanguishene to have some of their children baptized.

Mananowe, who was age fifteen years old at her marriage, presented her husband with a child, about every two years, until there were twelve children in the family, although five did not survive to adulthood. At their appropriate ages, both the boys and the girls were sent to Montreal to be educated after having been taught to speak, read and write English by their father.

In 1807, Ermatinger resigned from the North West Company, and by 1808, became an independent trader, as well as a merchant, at the Sault, on the north side of the river. He immediately became successful, perhaps in part because he had a very friendly agreement with his brother, Frederick, in Montreal, who regularly forwarded to him whatever merchandise was requested. Ermatinger started off with three employees but by 1812, he had fifty men in his employ.

W. Brian Stewart, in his book *The Ermatingers A 19th-Century Ojibway-Canadian Family* wrote, and provided references, to show that, in 1817, the Ermatinger brothers outfitted sixty employees, comprised of Mananowe's Ojibway relatives and friends, local Métis residents, as well as French

Canadians. No doubt, this fur trade venture provided a huge profit for Ermatinger.

Strangely, his former employer, the North West Company, that had a post in the Sault, did not object to Ermatinger's trade. Perhaps the incentive for the North West Company to remain quiet was because it purchased merchandise from him but of this reasoning, there is no proof.

When war with the Americans erupted in 1812, Ermatinger became a captain in the attack against Mackinac Island. In 1814, when everyone from the Sault and elsewhere was at Mackinac Island to defend an expected attempt by the Americans to take back Mackinac Island, Ermatinger stayed at the Sault. When, in 1814, the Americans were spotted sailing toward the Sault, Ermatinger, with the help of some of his employees, quickly buried all the furs he had. As it turned out, Ermatinger was the only Sault resident who had not gone to Mackinac Island to defend it. According to the author, Dr. John Bigsby, and as reported by Stewart, when Ermatinger was asked by the American commander, why he was at the Sault, instead of at Mackinac Island, Ermatinger responded that he was simply an honest man, trying to make a living while minding his own business. That was obviously the right answer because the Americans left him alone and did not burn his home.

It is not known why Ermatinger stayed home when everyone else had gone to Mackinac Island but it was definitely the right move on his part. Once the war was over, Ermatinger went back to trading, suffering no ill effects because of the war.

The Ermatinger children spent their early years in the Sault, spending their time with their Ojibway relatives, and Métis neighbours. At a time when racism was rampant in Montreal, these children did not suffer from being half white and half indigenous when, later, they were in Montreal.

In 1816, Ermatinger was appointed as justice of the peace for the Sault, an appointment that would have further elevated his standing in the community. When he was asked to go to Fort William, now Thunder Bay, Ontario, as justice of the peace, to arrest some Métis leaders who were to be charged with a number of murders, Ermatinger refused. It was thought that his refusal was because those to be charged had been friendly with the North West Company; therefore, he feared reprisals from that company, or perhaps he felt that Lord Selkirk was overreacting. There was another complication. Ermatinger had been supplying Selkirk's Red River Settlement for a number of years and kept doing so until 1821, or perhaps longer.

Over the years, Ermatinger built an exceptional business as is reflected in the stone home he had built for his family after the war of 1812, which still stands today. Apparently, he spent £2,000 on the building of the house, which was a vast amount of money at the time.

Ermatinger Old Stone House and Block House

By Sheri Minardi Photography

After the war, at the Sault, Ermatinger was the major competitor to the American, John Jacob Astor. For years, Ermatinger managed to circumvent American authorities while continuing to trade in the U.S. By late 1819, he could no longer acquire the appropriate licence.

As luck would have it, Ermatinger was able to buy Jean-Baptiste Nolin's post on the south side of the St. Marys River in 1819, which transaction helped Ermatinger enormously until 1822, when this property was expropriated by the U.S. military. All was not a total loss because Ermatinger did manage to obtain compensation for this property. Thereafter, he had to restrict his trade to the north side of the river, except that he still had a post on Drummond Island.

Ermatinger, with his father-in-law, travelled throughout their trading areas and it appears that both enjoyed a considerable profit. In addition, to Mananowe's Ojibway family, Ermatinger sent his employees on winter buying trips to Ojibway hunting sites although doing so cost him dearly.

By 1822, trade became more difficult to conduct with his Ojibway connections on the south side of the St. Marys River because the American military was occupying Sault, Michigan. Another complication came as a result of the merger of the North West Company and the Hudson's Bay Company which meant that the Sault was no longer on a major fur trade route, given the furs were now being taken northeast to James Bay and then transported out by ship. To top the problems off, a Canadian Customs Officer was placed at the Sault. This was extremely annoying because people had to pay a duty on everything bought in from the U.S.

As a general rule, Ermatinger sent his furs to Montreal by canoes and those canoes returned loaded with trade goods. Otherwise, he was known to send furs over the Great Lakes by schooner but it appears that this was rare.

Winter was a whirl of social activity at the Sault. Everyone on both sides of the river held dinners and parties, constantly, inviting anyone who was passing through the Sault, the military officers stationed on the U.S. side, John Siveright, a clerk with the Hudson's Bay post, fur traders, clerks, and anyone else who just happened to be there. The Ermatingers were always in the midst of this activity.

The only winter that the Ermatingers refrained from entertaining, other than a few dinners, was the winter of 1822 – 1823. Their son, George, had died in Montreal while at school. During the fall and winter, sons Edward and Lawrence died of dysentery at home. I gather that during the following winter, active social activities were resumed. For New Year's 1826, the Ermatingers entertained forty-seven men, thirty women, and seventy-five children.

By 1825, it was becoming difficult for Ermatinger to make a profit on the south side of the river so that he contemplated selling his post there to the American Fur Company. The last disaster to strike his business came when Drummond Island was given to the Americans in 1828. As a result, he had no choice but to sell that post to the Americans. This put an end to what had been Ermatinger's lucrative endeavours on Lake Superior's south side.

Ermatinger never owned the land upon which his house was situated on the north side of the river. The ownership of the Sault belonged to the Ojibway, and although the government of Upper Canada expected to purchase the land, had not done so.

In 1825, Ermatinger applied to the government for a deed of land but was not granted it. Later, upon Ermatinger's death, his eldest son, Charles Jr., inherited this house. Mananowe petitioned the government in 1847, and again in 1849, for a deed to the land but was unsuccessful. Charles Jr. never did acquire a deed to the land.

In 1852, Charles, Jr. leased the house to David and Margaret Pim, who operated a hotel on the premises, providing lodging and meals. Then, in 1853, Charles, Jr. quit deeded the house to the Pims for $3,000.

Over subsequent years, as reported by Stewart, the old stone house, as it is fondly called, went through various changes of use. It became a post office in 1858, operated initially by David Pim, and after his early death, by his wife, Margaret, until 1903. At one point, it was a courthouse as well as jail. The flip side of that usage was as a church. At another time, it was occupied as a tavern. Somewhere in its history, it became a dance hall. At another time, it was a respectable tea room, and at some point, an apartment building. After all these diverse changes, in 1964, the City of Sault Ste. Marie purchased the house and restored it to its former elegance. I think it would have been a blow to history had the City not acquired this exquisite home.

In 1827, his trade partner brother, Frederick, died. This meant that Charles inherited money and property on the Island of Montreal.

In 1828, at age fifty-two, Ermatinger retired, taking his wife and seven surviving children to Longue Pointe, a rural area of Montreal Island that was also close to the city. Based on the household items purchased for this home, it appears that the Ermatingers had expected to entertain on a grand scale.

As it transpired, they did not have the opulent dinners and parties with guests that they had anticipated and did not attend social events, merely because the social scene of his youth no longer existed. Stewart wrote that Ermatinger had commented in a letter to his daughter, living in York, that he was disappointed in the changes in Montreal's social practices. I believe Alexander Henry felt the same about Montreal when retired there.

Not much was written about Mananowe and I'm not sure why. Perhaps, she was a very shy, reserved person, or maybe she never learned to speak French or English since she was always able to communicate with her family in the Ojibway language.

It appears that her daughter, Frances, acted as hostess in their home in the Sault while her mother stayed in the background. Family letters indicate that she was a good mother who fondly cared for her children.

By 1830, his health was declining and Ermatinger died on September 4, 1833, at the age of fifty-seven years. Mananowe continued to live on the farm at Longue Point until she died in July, 1850, at about age sixty-five.

I highly recommend a visit to the Ermatinger Clergue National Historic Site at 800 Bay Street, in the Sault, to view replication of life as it was for the Sault's prominent residents from 1808 to 1870.

Autumn Shore of Batchewana Bay,
Lake Superior 2016

by Sheri Minardi Photography

Social Scene at the Sault 1814

The following letter, to George Gordon, North West Company clerk at Michipicoten describes the winter social scene at the Sault. It was written at Batchewana on February 11, 1812.

My Dear George

If I were not afraid that you will again fly into a passion, and scold and abuse me for neglect, I should certainly not write you this time having no news in the world to convey you. But you will right or wrong have me write; with, or without, a subject: be it so then to your own ....

I returned from St. Marie's the day before yesterday, whither I went the 27th ultimo. The day after I got there I went over with Mr. Logan to see Mr. Johnston. We were very politely received and invited to a ball at that gentleman's house the next day. You need not ask whether I went, and having gone, whether I had pleasure. In fact, he must be insensible to all delightful sensations who did not enjoy pleasure in the highest degree, in the company of a polite, cheerful and well-informed old man; of three or four jovial and sprightly young fellows; but above all of the most amiable set of fine girls that is to be seen between Montreal and the Rocky Mountain. We accordingly passed a most pleasant evening; drinking now and then a glass of jorum; dancing with and kissing the ladies till day-break. This was on Friday night.

On Sunday we had a grand dinner at Mr. Logan's where all the luxuries which the Sault affords were seen with profusion. After dinner a glass of wine to King George, our absent friends, and then a glass of jorum; while a cheerful and sentimental conversation enlivened the scene of mirth and made us forget all past and future sorrow. The day was concluded with an eloquent supper and a dish of tea with the ladies.

On Tuesday we had a grand ball at Mr. Logan's where all that the Sault contains of elegant and lovely were assembled. Again, there was drinking of jorum, dancing, but above all, kissing of the ladies. By the way, I must not forget to tell you I fell in love that night with Mademoiselle Magdeleine. This was the end of Tuesday's diversion.

On Wednesday we went to a sumptuous dinner at Mr. Johnston's, where nothing was spared that can render an entertainment delightful. The end of that was a supper with the ladies; and a great deal of sorrow on my part at taking leave of a certain young lady, who had almost made me forget Mademoiselle Magdeleine.

Thursday, we had a magnificent ball at Mr. Nolin's where jorum and the young ladies were in such profusion, and perfection, that it required a great deal of philosophy not to get intoxicated with the first or to fall in love with the last.

I must own it, my friend, it was there I met with my finishing blow; and fell beneath the charms of the lovely Mademoiselle Jorum.

Well, here is hurly burly for you. What now do you think of all that work?

For my part, I am now returned home, and just as lonesome as I was before and perhaps something worse.

No news as I told you already from the Sault, or any other place.

As soon as I shall get any I will write you a long letter.

In the meantime, farewell.

I remain as usual my dear George,

yours sincerely,

Frederick Goedike

The following details regarding the burning of the Sault in the war of 1812 – 1814 were taken from my book entitled American Attempt to Take Canada, War of 1812 – 1814, St. Joseph Island, Sault Ste. Marie.

The War of 1812 – 1814 was still on when on July 23, 1814, at least one quick thinking, fast paddling Indigenous fellow got to the Sault, beached his canoe, ran toward the North West Company holdings, located some Nor'westers, and emphatically explained that the Americans would be setting foot on their domain within the next two hours.

There was a major flurry of activity to get out of the Sault in the North West Company schooner, the *Perseverance*, but the wind was not blowing in the right direction.

Time flew by too quickly, so that before anyone could catch his breath, about 150 Americans swarmed the North West's buildings, while American Navy Lieutenant Turner made his way into Lake Superior.

Captain Robert McCargo and the crew of the *Perseverance* had, just prior to Turner's unwelcome appearance, abandoned the schooner, hopped into a canoe and paddled furiously to get away, heading north along the eastern side of Lake Superior to Fort William.

In the area of Michipicoten, the group met up with Gabriel Franchère, and others, coming from Fort William. McCargo told Franchère that he had set fire to the heavily loaded schooner before escaping.

After arriving at Fort William and reporting to the North West Company, McCargo left to sail the only remaining North West Company schooner, the *Recovery*, to Isle Royale, where he hid and camouflaged the ship in an inlet which is today called McCargo Cove.

Turner's letter to his superior, Captain Arthur Sinclair, dated July 28, 1814, while aboard the *Scorpion*, near Mackinac Island, stated that the crew had set a few fires throughout their schooner, and "scuttled" her. Scuttle usually means that they tried to sink her by opening a valve in the hull, or creating a hole in the bottom, to let water in, or perhaps, in this case, scuttle just meant that the ship was to be sunk by a blazing fire.

Turner continued to write that he got on board the *Perseverance*, put out the fires, and "secured her from sinking." He did not explain how he managed this.

He then wrote that because the wind was not in his favour, he could not try to get the ship over the rapids until the 26th. [In his letter to Lieutenant-Colonel George Croghan, Major Holmes stated the date as the 25th.] Turner described the rapids as follows:

> The fall in three-quarters of a mile
> is forty-five feet and the channel
> very rocky, the current runs from
> twenty to thirty knots, and in one
> place there is a perpendicular leap
> of ten feet between three rocks.

At the three rocks, the *Perseverance* "bilged," was moving fast, and landed beneath the rapids, on the shore, where she became flooded with water.

Turner then had the *Perseverance* set on fire.

I suspect that Turner had no experience whatsoever with turbulent rapids!

He further explained that his plan had been to get the ship safely down the rapids and load her with the contents of the storehouses, but instead had to settle for four "captured boats" containing Indigenous items.

The other items of value that were contained in four large buildings and two smaller ones were destroyed by fire. He noted that the goods had a value of between $50,000 and $100,000.

Fortunately, this was nowhere near the value of the furs expected to pass through the Sault sometime during the following month.

Normally food was stored at the Sault until it could be forwarded on to Fort William, but Turner did not specify what was contained in the buildings that belonged to the North West Company.

On the north side of the river - up in flames went all of the North West Company assets: their canal, canoe lock, and warehouses, although Turner only mentioned the warehouses in his letter.

Turner ended his letter by stating that "all private property was, according to your orders, respected."

This is in contrast to other reports that state that the huts of the fur traders were destroyed and private property was taken and later recovered when an American ship, the *Scorpion,* was captured near St. Joseph Island.

At the Sault, no one was around. Everyone available had gone to defend Mackinac. The Americans had a situation of no contest.

Holmes wrote to Lieutenant-Colonel Croghan, on July 27, 1814, from the *Scorpion*. He stated that he had arrived at the Sault on the 23rd and that the North West Agent had already escaped with a "considerable amount of goods."

How he could have known what goods had disappeared in one canoe, I cannot predict.

He confirmed that the *Perseverance* had been set on fire by her crew, and later "bilged" when Turner tried to bring her over the rapids.

Further, Holmes wrote that "most of the goods...were found in the woods on the American side." He concluded that the goods were owned by John Johnston, who was not present, and who he considered a traitor.

He stated that [Johnston's] "agent armed the Indians from his stores at our approach, and, lastly, because those goods, or a considerable part, were designed to be taken to Michilimackinac. Pork, salt, and groceries...." - he seized them.

He did not write that he had Johnston's home and other property destroyed by fire but many other references do state that Johnston's assets were completely burned.

Johnston's wife, Ozhah-guscodaywayquay, with all but one of her children, escaped to safety, and the remaining child was not harmed.

Later, the North West Company received some compensation from the British government, but poor Johnston experienced exasperation in trying to obtain compensation.

His assets were on the south side of the St. Marys, clearly American territory, but he was fighting for the British.

No deals were made with him by either government.

Luckily for Johnston, thirteen years later, his wife and children received American land grants.

Meanwhile, Lieutenant-Colonel McDouall, on Mackinac Island, wrote to Lieutenant Miller Worsley, on July 28, advising that the Americans were in his vicinity, that he was expecting to be attacked any day, describing the huge fleet of ships and their guns, and advising Worsley to get his ship, the *Nancy*, as far up Nottawasaga River as he could and construct a log building, containing six pounders, to defend the *Nancy*.

He knew that if the *Nancy* were captured, the people on Mackinac Island would starve during the following winter.

Captain Arthur Sinclair wrote his reporting letter to the U.S. Secretary of the Navy, from on board the *Niagara*, off of Mackinac Island, on July 29, 1814. He stated that "the capture of the *Perseverence* [*sic*] gave us the complete command of Lake Superior."

I cannot determine what he was thinking when he wrote this statement. He did not explain how he was going to get a ship into Lake Superior. He did not appear to be aware that the North West Company had another ship on Lake Superior.

He lamented that he had been required to go at Mackinac Island, instead of going into Lake Superior, writing that had he been in Lake Superior, he could have taken over all assets situated on that lake, as well as Fort William [now Thunder Bay, Ontario].

He felt that the fur trade would have been destroyed had he captured Fort William, given he believed that up to $2,000,000 worth of furs were at that fort at that time.

Further, he thought that severe damage had been done to Fort William, given the *Mink* and the *Perseverance*, with their loads of food supplies, would not be arriving, and he was convinced that those losses could not be replaced.

A group, comprised of Gabriel Franchère and three other men, arrived at the North West post at Batchewana, on July 29th, and was told by some women there, who kindly did the cooking for them, that the post clerk, Frederick Goedike, had gone to the Sault to see what was happening there.

The following day, Goedike arrived back and described to them the situation at the Sault. In Franchère's journal, he wrote that Goedike had told him that 150 Americans had "sacked and pillaged everything that seemed to them of value belonging to the North West Company and to a Mr. Johnston."

That same evening, William McGillivray arrived at Batchewana from Fort William.

The next day, everyone set out for the Sault to view the destruction of the North West Company assets.

Franchère wrote that "The sawmills, warehouses, houses and so forth had all been destroyed and were still smoking." The schooner was at the foot of the rapids, completely burned.

Then, he and the others with him began creating a "defensive position" but he did not describe it. Upon approach, some Indigenous people who were camped nearby, agreed to help if needed.

Meanwhile, McGillivray's food supply had dwindled so that his group was reduced to two meals per day.

McGillivray had sent an express canoe to Mackinac Island, on August 1st, to let McDouall know what had transpired at the Sault; however, the messenger returned from Mackinac Island, on August 4th, to advise that it had not been safe to approach that island because it was surrounded by American ships.

Franchère reported that McGillivray's group found Charles Ermatinger, "who had an attractive establishment. He had just finished building a windmill to encourage agriculture . . ." Ermatinger showed them the wheat, growing there, that was three or four feet tall, as well as other grains.

Then, everyone went over to the south side of the river to view the damage there. Franchère wrote, regarding Nolin, "His house had an air of opulence and still bore traces of grandeur, which showed that he had formerly lived in considerable comfort."

Franchère's next journal entry stated that they heard about the American attack on Mackinac Island.

By August 19th, they were still at the Sault when two North West Company agents arrived from Fort William, in advance of canoes carrying a vast amount of fine furs valued at not less than $1,000,000.

Two days later, Franchère left for the mouth of the French River, with an advance group who were to check the route for Americans.

Heavily armed men, numbering between 325 and 335, travelling in forty-four large canoes, arrived at the mouth of the French River during the evening of August 25, 1814, and from there proceeded to Montreal without incident.

As an aside, Franchère was the trader and merchant for the American Fur Company in Sault Ste. Marie, Michigan, from 1834 to about 1842, where he resided with his wife and children.

Warriors joined the British against the Americans in the war of 1812 - 1814 because the British promised to take care of the Indians. The Indians said: "no, it's our land, we'll take care of you." The British promised to protect the Indians' rights, respect their lands, and not interfere with fishing and hunting practices. This is not how things turned out.

Chief Dean Sayers, of Batchewana, advised that six hundred warriors from the area of the Sault fought in the war, both here and in southern Ontario.

A vast number of warriors also came from the U.S. to fight for the British. One of them was my ancestor, Tecumseh, who was already battle hardened due to having fought the settlers in the

U.S. who thought they had the right to take over Ohio, and other areas.

Batchewana Chief Wabechechake was killed, in 1813, at Fort George in the Niagara Falls area

Chief Shingwauk took part in the war, fighting beside General Brock who, just before he was killed, gave his sword to Chief Shingwauk. Unfortunately, in later years, the sword was contained in a building at Garden River that burned to the ground. Somehow during this sad event, the sword went missing. I believe Brock also gave Shingwauk the epaulettes from his uniform.

Having studied the war of 1812 thoroughly, I know that without the Indigenous warriors, we would have become another U.S. state by losing the war.

At about age seventy years, encouraged by Henry Rowe Schoolcraft, Jean Baptiste Perrault prepared a narrative of his life as a voyageur His narrative is with the Schoolcraft Manuscripts in the Smithsonian Institute at Washington. From his narrative, I chose the following details.

Perrault departed Montreal on the 28th of May, 1783, at the age of twenty-two years, to develop a job for himself as a fur trader. Throughout his career, he travelled through vast areas, continuing until his retirement in 1821, at age sixty years. Between 1787 and 1793, he was an independent fur trader. In 1793, he joined the North West Company but did not find that company to be honourable towards its employees which led him to state: "It must be said that the North West Company was then legislator and king, hanged, stole, and violated, etc. The extent of their crimes was close to the limit."

Perrault had been a clerk in the fur trade, working for John Sayer, in the Lake Superior area but during the war of 1812 – 1814, he was at Kingston, Ontario.

Post-war, the North West Company hired him to reconstruct buildings that had been destroyed at the Sault during the war. He accepted this task as a master carpenter because he felt that his earnings otherwise were too meagre to support his family. He arrived in the Sault in about April of 1815, for a period of two years, and during that time, with the help of five skilled men, built a saw-mill, houses, stores, powder magazine, and other buildings.

Upon completion, when he asked for his pay from Mr. McGillis who was at the Sault, Perrault was informed that he would have to travel to Montreal to collect his pay and if he did not, he would forfeit his compensation. Well, I can see in this situation why he had made such a negative comment about the North West Company. Perrault secured a place in one of Mr. Ermatinger's boats and proceeded to Montreal, leaving the Sault on August 7th, 1817 and arriving at his destination on August 20th. I would say, travelling by canoe, that excellent time was made. I cannot imagine canoeing all the way to Montreal within fourteen days but that is accurate information. He collected his pay but with much difficulty and inconvenience to himself. The Company advised him that the rules had changed and he would only be paid after he had been in Montreal for one month. As the river travelling season was nearing an end for the year, he was prevented from promptly returning to the Sault. One complication led to another so that he was forced to spend the winter near Laval. Finally, after missing a few opportunities to travel with others to the Sault, he purchased supplies and set out on his own. A brave and dangerous undertaking for anyone. He left on the 1st of August, 1818, and arrived at Mr. Johnston's house, in the Sault, unscathed, on the 31st.

Prior to leaving the Sault for Montreal, Perrault had contracted with the Hudson Bay Company to move his family to Michipicoten where he would work. However, upon his return from

Montreal, for some unknown reason, he did not have a canoe, which meant that he had to spend the winter at the post at the Sault. Fortunately, Mr. Souliere, of the Sault, agreed that Perrault and his family could occupy his house.

During January, Perrault, along with his son, William, travelled to Drummond Island to conduct business with Mr. Solomon. I imagine that they must have snowshoed to Drummond. While there, he contracted with Mr. La Croix to build a saw-mill for him. This was good news for his income so that he returned to the Sault, packed up his family, and took them with him on February 17, 1819. By July 20th, he had completed his work and therefore returned to the Sault.

Perrault then made preparations to go to Michipicoten. He did not leave immediately as his daughter, Suzanne's birth was imminent, and he wanted to allow his wife one month following the birth to recover, without travel. As a result, the family did not leave the Sault until the beginning of September, which was very late to commence travel on Lake Superior.

Upon leaving the Sault, they camped at Point aux Pins for an unspecified number of days to pick blueberries, given that a particularly abundant crop was in bloom. It appears to me that they must have stayed here until the beginning of October.

Perrault stated that it then took one month to travel to Michipicoten due to being restrained by strong winds. At one point, they nearly starved and ate bark from the birch trees.

The family arrived at Michipicoten on November 2nd but found that many disagreements between the men of the Hudson's Bay Company and the North West Company had caused the abandonment of fur trading with the Indigenous people at this post about two years prior. A small station was maintained for forwarding correspondence onward and as a stop for the colonists heading to the Red River.

Perreault set out, with one other employee, on May 16th, on a sixteen-day trip which appeared to be to deliver mail but I could not determine exactly where they went, but it appears that they travelled east to Brunswick House which was in the area of present-day Chapleau.

In July, Perrault was asked to make two canoes for Governor Vincent of the Hudson's Bay Company. While getting ready to do this, Mr. Stuart sent a barge to the Sault to obtain supplies for the Michipicoten post. Perrault's Indigenous wife, who is not named, but I believe she was Marie Hayes, travelled on the barge with Doctor Boun [sic] and young Suzanne Perrault, to the Sault. Suzanne died a few days after arriving at the Sault. The barge returned to Michipicoten in early August with Mrs. Perrault, who brought along another daughter, Esther, about age sixteen years, who had been left with Mr. Johnston the year before. There was no explanation as to why Esther had been living in the Sault.

Thereafter, Perrault made another canoe for fishing and spent the remainder of his time fishing at Michipicoten, mainly for white fish and the salting of same. Otherwise, he was kept busy dealing with the snares to catch partridges. Overall, he reported that the winter allowed for pleasant living conditions.

By May of 1821, the canoes arriving from Montreal advised him that the North West Company no longer had authority and had amalgamated with the Hudson's Bay Company. The rules for the traders were no longer as they had been. There would be few privileges for the traders and, in particular, regarding their families and moving expenses. With this news, Perrault tendered his resignation because his employment conditions would not be favourable for his large family.

The Perrault family departed Michipicoten on June 29th, 1821, arriving at the Sault on July 6th, where the family permanently settled. It is not clear what occupied his time during his retirement at the Sault but he was a skilled carpenter and a fisherman, so I expect he passed his time productively, without having to move his family again. Perrault had been a fur trader and voyageur for his adult life and was now sixty years of age.

In addition, he had spent two years as a teacher at some point during his long career.

Jean Baptiste Perrault died at Sault, Ontario, at age eighty-three years.

Shooting Rapids   (Quebec)

Painter: Frances Anne Hopkins (1838 – 1919).
Library and Archives Canada, Acc. No. 1989-401-2.
Licensed under Public Domain via Commons –
https://wiki2.org/en/

James Hargrave

Hargrave, from Scotland, served his first year as an apprentice clerk at the Sault from 1820 – 1821. He was then sent to Thunder Bay, followed by York Factory which became his normal post. In the summer of 1851, he travelled by land from York Factory to the Sault. Here, his work was to supply provisions to the areas of Lakes Huron and Superior. The following summer, his wife, Letitia Mactavish, joined him in the Sault. Apparently, he was strict in conducting business which really annoyed his American customers. For some unknown reason, his personal expenses were a lot higher than expected which did not make for a happy man. His wife and one child died in the fall of 1854 which severely added to his sorrows. In the summer of 1855, James Hargrave left the Sault for the final time.

The Merger

Upon the merger of the North West Company with the Hudson's Bay Company, the post at the Sault conducted business under the Hudson's Bay Company but there was very little fur trade activity. Michipicoten became the important centre for the fur trade because the furs were transported from there by land travel to James Bay to then be taken to England by ships.

Hudson's Bay Post, Sault Ste. Marie, 1863
Painting by William Armstrong (1822 – 1914)
www.torontopubliclibrary.ca
JRR 2426 Cab IV (Armstrong) Rights and Licenses:
Public Domain

The Sault Becomes Two Countries 1820

Pursuant to the Jay Treaty of 1794, the south side of the St. Marys River became American and the north side Canadian. No one paid attention to the border until 1820, when the Lewis Cass Expedition, arrived to survey the area, following which, in 1822, Fort Brady was built where De Repentigny's fort had been.

In 1820, on the American side, were about twenty buildings. Over on the Canadian side of the St. Marys River, there were perhaps a half a dozen, where Métis children resided with their parents who were mainly French, with some English.

By the middle of the 1830s, the people living in the Sault, Ontario had become independent of the Hudson's Bay Company and actually sold supplies and provisions to the Hudson's Bay Company instead of purchasing from it. The inhabitants had also created a business in fishing and sold salted fish to markets further south. The men had become skilled tradesmen, able to earn good pay for their labour, but the Hudson's Bay Company did not want to pay what the men asked so did not hire them.

By 1843, the Hudson's Bay Company had very little activity in its post at the Sault and completely closed its operations in the Sault in 1869.

The former employees, consisting of Indigenous people and Métis, continued to live in an area close to the rapids, which became for a long time, known as a French neighbourhood. In due course, it had a French church and school, side by side, both named St. Ignatius, on what is now Cathcart Street. I have not been able to determine when the French speaking Catholic Church and school came into being. It may have been that they were replaced at some point with modern buildings. Although I attended an English speaking elementary school in the Sault, my Saturdays were spent at St. Ignatius French speaking school. We were taught French by the Grey Sisters, and I thoroughly enjoyed my time there and was very sad to see the school demolished in 2005.

Religion in the Sault

In 1831, Father Frederic Baraga, a Jesuit priest, came to Michigan and was kept quite busy on both sides of the St. Marys River, as well as north of Lakes Huron and Superior. He was an accomplished man, learning the Ojibway language, publishing books of Ojibway grammar, Ojibway dictionary, and in about 1832, published a prayer book in Ojibway. Baraga was known as the snowshoe priest, travelling about 700 miles during the winter to vast areas.

By 1846, there was a Jesuit missionary post in Sault, Ontario that was replaced in 1875 and dedicated in 1876, as the Parish Church of the Sacred Heart. It was renamed in 1936 as the Cathedral of the Precious Blood which is located on Queen Street East. There are now various Catholic churches throughout the Sault.

The Anglican religion was brought to the Sault, in 1832, by Rev. William McMurray as written by Richard E. Ruggle in the *Dictionary of Canadian Biography*. McMurray had been born in 1810, in Armagh County, in N. Ireland.

In about 1831, he married John Johnston's daughter, Charlotte, who was also the granddaughter of an Ojibway chief. She acted as interpreter for her husband, as well as taught Indigenous women to sing Anglican hymns. Rev. McMurray translated the Anglican catechism into Ojibway which was printed in 1834. After McMurray left, Chief Shingwauk provided Anglican lessons and hymns to the Garden River Indigenous.

In 1883, the Ojibway First Nation of Garden River, in conjunction with the Anglican Church, built a chapel on what is now Queen Street East, which is known as Bishop Fauquier Chapel. It is now 135 years old.

The mid to late 1800s brought a strong Presbyterian presence to this area which was comprised of many settlers of Scotch-Irish ancestry who had originally been from Northern Ireland. Many had lived elsewhere in Ontario before relocating to the Sault. Also, many Calvinist Methodists are listed in the censuses of 1861, 1871, and 1881.

In 1925, three Protestants churches, being Presbyterian, Methodist, and Congregationalist, amalgamated to form the United Church of Canada.

In about 1900, the Jewish people of the Sault established Congregation Beth Jacob, unaffiliated. In 1901, there were eight Jews in the Sault, and by 1911, eighty were noted in the local census. There were Jews in Sault, MI, who formed a close relationship with those of Sault, ON, and come over to attend religious services. Initially, they met above their stores on Queen Street East but their synagogue has existed on Bruce Street since 1946.

Numerous other religions now co-exist in the Sault with the various Christian denominations: Traditional Aboriginal Spirituality, Hindu, and Buddhist. Perhaps the newest is the Islamic Association.

1850 Robinson Huron Treaty

This treaty transferred vast amounts of Ojibway lands to the Canadian government. The Ojibway owned Sault, Ontario, but the federal government insisted on having it so that the Ojibway were told to move to Manitoulin Island. Shingwauk refused. After thousands of years of living in the Sault, the Indians had to move down the river. How silly is that? So, in 1841, Garden River was created. The treaty described the lands which made up the reserves to be set aside for the use of the Indigenous people.

One part of the treaty stated that every Indian was to be given $2 per year. An Indian Affairs representative would travel to each reserve annually, accompanied by an RCMP officer, to hand out the $2. I wonder if the RCMP was on hand in case the Indians decided to revolt and strangle the government's agent. As at 2018, each status Indian is given $4 per year. According to inflation statistics, the government still is not being honest because today that original sum of $2 is now $60.24. So, we can see that $60 is not going to make anyone wealthy; however, this is a clear example of the government not honouring the treaty.

Lyle Sayers, retired long-time chief of Garden River, told me that Indians were not allowed to vote in federal elections until 1962. This, notwithstanding they had fought for Canada in every war Canada was ever engaged in.

Sayers also described that up to the early 1960s, every Garden River Council meeting had to be chaired by a government Indian Agent. In 1964, Dick Pine was having no more of this. He told the Indian Agent to go and sit in the corner because he was (rightly) taking his chair.

This is a very basic example of the government attempting to hold the Indians down so as not to progress. Some nerve! So, there have been struggles between the Indigenous and the Canadian government. There will be ongoing negotiations between all Canadian Indigenous people and Canada in an effort to gain Indigenous rights.

As an aside, Sayers explained that the surnames of the local Indians were taken from names that existed in the area, such as Sayers and Nolin. The new names came as a result of the Indians having very long names that Canada's agents could not spell.

Garden River is to the east of Sault, Ontario, and Batchewana is located on White Fish Island and in a small area east of the city, but more so to the north.

Shingwauk Residential School

This school for Indigenous students existed over a period of ninety-seven years, from 1873 to 1970. I noticed in the 1911 census report that the students attending the Shingwauk Residential School were listed as being "Anglican" and that the people in charge were all Anglicans, from England. Those children had their own religious beliefs but were forced to accept Anglicanism.

I was horrified to read that the children were listed as "inmates." The definition of an inmate is a person confined to an institution such as a prison. Synonyms are: prisoner, convict, captive. The children in residential schools clearly suffered mental, emotional and physical cruelty, but seeing in the official government census report that they were designated as "inmates" really made me ashamed of Canada to permit this designation.

Upon looking at the school photos, I noticed that all the girls had the exact same haircut which was a blunt cut at about chin length, with bangs. The people in charge were controlling, to put it mildly.

From reading about the school, it became apparent to me that its aim was to stomp on individuality until it was completely destroyed.

Growing Pains

Until 1887, the Sault was dependent on water for travel, mail, and shipment of products. During the winter months, the Sault was isolated when water traffic had to shut down. By that year, the Canadian Pacific Railway had constructed a rail line to connect the Sault with Sudbury, and at Sudbury, passengers could change trains to continue on elsewhere. By 1889, people of the Sault could ride the rails to anywhere in Canada via Sudbury. The International Rail Bridge was also completed in 1887, between the twin Saults, which created the opportunity to move into vast areas of the U.S.A. The Canadian canal, constructed between 1889 and 1895, allowed iron ore and other necessities to pass from Lake Superior into the St. Marys River and onward.

By 1892, the Sault had telephone and electricity. It was at this point that the town's population began to grow.

1891 Census

In this report, residents listed the following as places of birth: Russia, Germany, Italy, Sweden, Iceland, France, Ireland, Scotland, England, U.S.A., Quebec and Nova Scotia. Russians were all listed as working on the canal. By 1911, the census report also listed people having been born in Wales, Austria, and Holland.

Hydroelectric Plant

I include reference to the magnificent, one-quarter mile width structure on the American side of the St. Marys River because anytime I have a visitor to the Sault, and we look across the river, the first question that is always asked is: what is that beautiful building right beside the water?

That gorgeous building, made of sandstone, was built between 1898 and 1902. It has had various corporate ownership changes since it was constructed by Francis H. Clergue as a powerhouse. When I was a child, it was Union Carbide, and then Edison Sault. This powerhouse is now owned by Cloverland Electric Cooperative. I would recommend www.powermag.com which has much detail regarding this hydroelectric plant. Lake Superior State University operates, on the east side of the building, an aquatic research laboratory.

When it became apparent that the Sault was on the verge of creating industry and, therefore, attracting more people, the question became what to do about a hospital. The local municipal government was not in a position to finance a hospital. Upon inquiries, both the federal and provincial governments refused to contribute. According to Elizabeth A. Iles, in her book entitled *Ask the Grey Sisters Sault Ste. Marie and the General Hospital, 1898 – 1998*, T.F Chamberlain, who was on a short visit to the Sault, told the hospital committee, "if you wish a hospital of which the work is serious and lasting, ask the Grey Sisters."

On June 29, 1897, Dr. Robert J. Gibson of the Sault, made contact with one of the Grey Sisters, Sister St. Syprien, at St. Joseph's Hospital in Sudbury, by writing to her to explain that a hospital was needed in the Sault.

The Jesuit priest, J. A. Primeau, at the Sault's Sacred Heart church, also wrote to Superior General Demers, and stated: "the citizens, in great majority Protestant, are strongly in favour of a hospital established by the sisters and are disposed to assist."

By May of 1898, Dr. Gibson presented to city council the Grey Sisters proposal to build a hospital. The council agreed to the proposal and a committee was created to determine a site for the hospital. By June, 1898, the Grey Sisters decided to rent a house, as a temporary hospital, to immediately begin their work.

Very soon, three riverfront lots of land were purchased by the Sisters for the hospital to be constructed.

Two Grey Sisters, Marie du Sauveur and Ste. Rosalie, arrived in the Sault, from Ottawa, by train, on September 13, 1898. They immediately got to work to turn the rented house into a temporary hospital. The house was located on Water Street, which is now called Bay Street, that was situated very close to the Ermatinger old stone house, near Pim Street.

Ten days after arrival, the Sisters began treating their first patient who had typhoid. Two days later, another typhoid patient arrived. Given typhoid was such a feared disease, the Sisters could not obtain help from anyone to assist with the laundry. Undaunted by the illness, the Sisters washed items at night and the sheets were placed around the stove to dry.

The house was far from ideal given there was frost on the walls during the winter, and water had to be carried in barrels from the river. To top it off, there was next to no space for the Sisters to live.

The work of the Sisters was phenomenal. While occupying this shabby environment, they treated 64 patients.

In due course, in 1899, the hospital on Queen Street was ready. Dr. Gibson, in charge of the opening ceremony, stated that although "the institution would be under the management of the Sisters, its doors would be open to the black and white, the rich and poor, the Protestant and Catholic alike...."

The hospital progressed to such an extent that by 1902, it was overcrowded so that in 1908, a wing was added which made the building twice its original size.

Sister Ste. Constance wrote the following which had been translated from French to English.

It happened . . . in 1908 . . . the mission was very poor; the revenue didn't cover the expenses......So there was always a large number of immigrants – Finnish, Polish, Russian – who were all admitted for free . . . We had to find ways to remedy this problem. We held country fairs, raffles etc. in the summer but it wasn't enough. Therefore, in winter, funds were collected from the churches and the lumber camps: The lumber camps were the most encouraging because they brought in sums of $1,500 to $1,800. But what sacrifices on these excursions. First, the cold and all sorts of inconveniences. . . . Here is an experience that should have cost us our lives. One beautiful morning, we had decided to walk to the neighboring lumber camp two miles away, saving us two days. We were following the railway tracks because the train wasn't scheduled to pass that day so we had nothing to fear. While walking we said our rosary. The path was winding and the railway tracks snow-covered, it was as if we had been thrust between two huge mountains, the path very narrow. We had just crossed over the "footbridge" which is extremely long when suddenly a machine fast approached us. It was a snow blower. Like a bolt of lightning we each threw ourselves onto the sides of the track sinking up to our necks in the snowy void 15 – 20 feet deep. Each thought the other was dead. Finally, with great difficulty, I climbed out to go to the aid of my companion who wasn't able to free herself; she couldn't see a thing because her glasses were frosted. The Lord's very special protection was with us for we had no injuries except that we shook with fear until the next day. . . . We found the way long. . . . We continued on our way and arrived at the exact lumber camp we were looking for . . . It was the Alabama lumber camp in Blind River in February of 1908. It was the last stop before taking the road back to the Sault. What luck! . . . There were 300 men at the camp. All of them were Protestant. After supper we went to the lumberjacks' camp. They were sitting around the big hall, also the dormitory, lined with bunk beds, waiting for us. Seeing them sitting on the edge of their beds, their legs dangling, gave you a little chill when you entered. Soon, they put you at ease because they were polite. . . . Each lumberjack gave his name and the amount he wanted to give; we collected almost $400. The rounds took a good two hours because the men all had questions to ask us: our name; where we came from; what we did; how long we had been in the convent; if we were "finisher sisters." They could not understand that we would never be returning home to our families. After the rounds, we returned to the office for the Bourgeois to write us a cheque; we never kept cash on us. The evening lasted well until 11:00 . . .

(Author's note: They slept in the office)
...it was a one-room, small building, 15 by 15. In the centre was the stove made of timber with the joints held together by soil and moss. The inside walls were covered with black felt-lined paper to break the wind. In a corner, were two bunk beds made of rough boards fitted with hay and covered with gray wool blankets. In another corner the assistant's office, a counter, a desk and on the wall were fairly large shelves where the items for sale were placed: blankets, sweaters, moccasins, mittens, etc. On the other side was a table on which were found a cauldron of water, a basin, some soap and a towel. A huge lamp hung from the ceiling while mittens and toques hung on sticks to dry.

In 1902, telephone service was added. Today, it is difficult to imagine a building without telephones.

Eventually, the General Hospital, after many additions and changes incorporated with the Plummer Memorial Hospital.

Fishing on the Ste. Mary's River in 1901

Wikimedia Commons, the free media repository

Voyageurs on the rapids

© Library and Archives Canada

Twentieth Century

Language Problems

By 1926, the Grey Sisters were divided into three sections: two English speaking and one French. The Vatican sent out a notice that the Grey Nuns of the Cross (Sisters of Charity) at the Sault hospital, who spoke French, were to be replaced by the newly created English speaking Grey Sisters of the Immaculate Conception. Historically, it has often happened that a decision overseas affected people on this continent, although by 1926, the Sault had transformed to an English speaking society.

The French Nuns were very sad to leave, but no doubt, those indomitable Sisters were given handshakes with warm expressions of thanks, as they were sent on their way.

The fact is, these French Grey Sisters had masterminded the success of the General Hospital, had physically worked to exhaustion, and were not originally from the Sault but still came and gave their all.

Plummer Memorial Hospital

By 1906, discussions began among a group of non-Catholics, to establish a public hospital. As a child, I personally knew Frank J. Davey, who was in the lead in this endeavour. Without a doubt, he was a progressive, honourable man, who accomplished much for the Sault; however, at that time, I know there was a strong divide between Protestants and Catholics.

In 1917, the group opened the Royal Victoria Hospital, an eighteen-bed hospital in a house at 137 Albert Street East.

The family of the late WH. Plummer, in 1920, donated their home, called Lynnhurst, on Queen Street East, very close to the General Hospital, to be used as a hospital. The hospital from Albert Street then moved to Queen Street. Initially, this hospital had the name Royal Victoria but was changed to the Plummer Memorial Public Hospital.

Sault Area Hospitals

Chamberlain, who had suggested contacting the Grey Sisters was back in 1897, and at that time, stated: "One good, well-equipped hospital sufficiently large to accommodate the sick of its locality, can do more and better work than two more small hospitals, as, where duplicated in this way, the tendency is to divide the community in its philanthropic work and cause a waste of money in keeping up an extra building, staff of officers, etc." How true his words were.

Eventually, the General Hospital and the Plummer Memorial Hospital amalgamated, and much later, in 2011, one new state-of-the-art hospital, named the Sault Area Hospitals, opened on Great Northern Road at the Third Line.

A very notable fact about this new hospital is that it was given close to $60,000,000 in donations. For a small city, having a population of about 75,000, that is a phenomenal amount of money.

My own opinion is that the Sault has come a long way from its twentieth century history of dividing itself along religious lines and is to be commended for so doing.

Entrepreneur Francis H. Clergue

As reported in the City of Sault Ste. Marie, Ontario, website, www.cityssm.on.ca/library it was through a chance meeting on the train to Toronto that two lawyers from the Sault struck up a conversation with H.B. Foster of Bangor, Maine. The conversation turned to the production of hydroelectricity at the Sault, using the rapids of the St. Marys River. As it turned out, Foster knew Francis H. Clergue, an entrepreneur, who had the financial backing of a group in Philadelphia. One conversation led to another and then to correspondence and in due course the arrival at the Sault of Clergue. He presented his proposal to the town and then its citizens, all the while offering a very lucrative financial package. It was an offer that could not be overlooked. By October, 1894, the parties had entered into written agreements which gave Clergue a franchise for water and electricity. True to his word, Clergue created a system that provided the Sault with plenty of electricity. I dare say that the cost of electricity has never entered the minds of the people of the Sault until recent years.

Clergue became the founder of St. Mary's Paper mill that was built on the land where the old North West Company post had been situated. The mill produced pulp and paper, remaining in operation, through various changes in corporate ownership until 2011, when it was determined that the business was no longer viable. Fortunately, the mill's beautiful sandstone building has been refurbished for cultural purposes.

The steel plant, as well as a portion of the Algoma Central Railway extending northward to connect with the transcontinental railroad, and the Helen mine at Michipicoten, were all masterminded by Clergue.

By 1903, Clergue was in over his head financially. Fortunately, the various enterprises that he started did continue under new management.

Sir James Dunn to the Rescue

Sir James Dunn's relationship with the Sault began when he became one of the liquidators of the bankrupt Clergue companies, according to an article in the April 16, 2017 edition of www.sootoday.com, provided by the Sault Ste. Marie Public Library and its Archives. Due to his efforts, with British investors, the steel plant was saved from closure. Financial trouble struck the steel plant again in 1932 when it declared bankruptcy and stopped its operations. The mayor of the Sault requested that Dunn lend his expertise to save the steel plant. He saved the plant two years later and this time, held vast financial control himself. His efforts resulted in success in that the steel plant then produced fifty percent of the pig-iron in Canada and one-third of the steel in Canada. Apart from his involvement with industry, financially, he supported the hospital in the Sault and created a scholarship for high-achieving secondary school students which were much relied upon to pursue a university education.

Soo Locks-Sault-Ste Marie

by U.S. Army Corps of Engineers soldier or
employee -
http://www.lre.usace.army.mil/newsandevents/pu
blications/publications/soolocks-saultste-
marie/aerialpicture2/. Licensed under Public
Domain via Commons -
https://wiki2.org/en/File:Soo_Locks-Sault-
Ste_Marie.png#/media/File:Soo_Locks-Sault-
Ste_Marie.png

WW I

Who would have thought that there would be any Nazi German interest in the Sault prior to and during World War I? According to *The Border at Sault Ste. Marie*, by Graeme S. Mount, John Abbott, and Michael J. Mulloy, there was a fellow living in Sault, Canada, in 1915, who was a German draftsman. His brother in the U.S. reported him missing and asked the German consulate in the U.S. to look into his disappearance.

The U.S. consulate in Sault, Ontario was contacted and discovered that the draftsman was in the Canadian Sault, but it does not appear to have provided information about him to the German consulate. In Sault, Canada, he had been arrested upon the knowledge that he had created drawings of the locks on both sides of the St. Marys River, as well as the International Rail Bridge that passed above the locks, and various other railroad bridges in the area. Apparently, he went to the trouble of having them mailed from New York to Germany. He was jailed, and nothing happened as a result of his endeavours.

Many men from the Sault and area joined the war effort and fought valiantly overseas earning Canada its recognition as a nation. As a result of Canada's extreme sacrifice, it signed the Peace Treaty, in its own right, not as a colony of Britain.

My father told me that the locks had to be protected during World War II because it was imperative to get iron ore to steel plants to manufacture war machinery as well as transport wheat from the west. There was fear that Nazi Germany could send ships into James Bay, to the northeast, or fly from occupied Norway, across the north, and then southward to attack the locks.

In *City of the Rapids: Sault Ste. Marie's Heritage*, by Bernie Arbic, of Sault, Michigan, he wrote that in March, 1942, the 399th Barrage Balloon Battalion reported to Sault, Michigan. Out of 7,000 to 7,300 men assigned to the Sault Military District, about nine hundred were stationed in Sault, Ontario. In addition, radar sites were established as far as 300 miles north of the Sault. Basically, defence of the twin Saults incorporated searchlights, anti-aircraft guns, as well as barrage balloons. Eventually, it was decided that there was little threat to the area so that the Barrage Balloon Battalion moved out.

Meanwhile, in Canada, thousands of men and women had either volunteered or were conscripted for the war effort. I had an uncle, Allan Rousseau, who was trained, as a rifleman, to be part of a force that would eventually attack Japan; however, in the meantime, he was sent elsewhere, and the dropping of the atomic bombs by the U.S. ended the plan to invade Japan.

He was sent to Kiska, near Alaska, as part of a joint U.S.-Canadian effort to dislodge the Japanese who were occupying Kiska. This plan was kept a secret to such an extent that the soldiers did not know where they were going until aboard ships heading north from the west coast towards Kiska. The Japanese evacuated the island, under cover of fog and darkness, so the soldiers were spared a battle; however, they were required to remain there for five months. During their stay, the soldiers experienced the worst weather conditions endured by the Canadian Army anywhere, throughout its entire history.

Next, Allan was with the Argylls when they fought their way into Germany during the last month of the war.

At the end of January, 1946, he returned home to St. Joseph Island, safe and sound, and for him, life went on.

Lyle Sayers explained to me that the many Indians who signed up to fight in both wars had to give up their Indian Status to do so. That is to say, they became 'white men.' After the wars were over, these newly created 'white men' were not allowed into pubs to have a drink with their former comrades-in-arms because once again they were considered Indians, notwithstanding they no longer had Indian status.

When will Canada ever learn!

Super Moon and Game Night

By Sheri Minardi Photography

The tower, with beacon, is a memorial to all those who served in wars for Canada.

It is situated on the arena property where the Sault Greyhounds play hockey.

Group of Seven

The most famous artists of Canada, whose Canadian landscape oil paintings sell for millions of dollars, created many of their works of art in Algoma, and in particular, along the Algoma Central Railway. They travelled along the railway in a boxcar, with the inside transformed into a living space. At particular rail sidings along the way, their home on steel wheels was parked. They, then, hiked or canoed throughout the scenery while creating their timeless works of art.

Local history states that the members of the group who frequented Algoma from 1918 – 1923 were Lawren Harris, A.Y. Jackson, Franz Johnston, J.E.H. MacDonald and Arthur Lismer.

According to David P. Silcox, in his book entitled *The Group of Seven and Tom Thomson*, Lawren Harris first travelled the ACR in May, 1918, looking for dramatic, austere and wild landscapes. These he discovered at the rivers Agawa, Montreal, and Batchewana, as well as Agawa Canyon. Silcox quotes a paragraph from Jackson's autobiography wherein Jackson stated: "I know of no more impressive scenery in Canada for the landscape painter." Silcox wrote that Jackson had recalled in his autobiography that travel was also via "a three-wheel jigger." It had two railway wheels on one track, and one railroad wheel on the opposite track. It was moved along the track by pushing up and down on an arm, attached to the base. It was quite small, sort of like a bike on train wheels, and provided no protection against the weather.

The group consisted of J.E.J. MacDonald, Arthur Lismer, Frederick Varley, Franz Johnston, who left the group in 1921, Franklin Carmichael, Lawren Harris, and Tom Thomson. The group received financial support from Lawren Harris who was heir to the Massey-Harris farm machinery fortune, as well as support from Dr. James MacCallum. During the WW I, both Jackson and Varley were official war artists. Their art is displayed at the Art Gallery of Algoma and the McMichael Canadian Art Collection in Kleinburg, Ontario.

Anyone who is a fan of The Group of Seven paintings would thoroughly enjoy the Agawa Canyon Tour Train ride.

Agawa Canyon

A place dear to my heart is the Agawa Canyon, accessible by travelling the Algoma Central Railway. My father was a locomotive engineer for the ACR so that I had many train trips between the Sault and Hearst as a child.

The canyon is a favourite destination for tourists due to the spectacular scenery, especially during the autumn season. I travelled through Switzerland and Austria, both of which have breathtaking, dramatic scenery, but the beauty of Algoma is another type of magnificent beauty.

I discovered a delightful book, by Norma C. Norman, entitled *The Canyon Years 1925 – 1941*. This is a book about a family who resided at Agawa Canyon both, before and during, the Great Depression of the 1930s. Norman described the living conditions which included winter temperatures from – 40 to – 60 degrees F. without electricity, plumbing, and insulation. The heat was generated from a cast iron heater. There was frozen water in the house, in a bucket, every winter morning. There were times when the train snowplow passed by the front porch of the house and filled it with snow which meant that Norman's father had to climb out of a second-storey window to dig the snow away from the front door before anyone could exit the house.

There was no chance of popping into a local grocery store to pick up a few necessities. Norman described that her mother wrote the grocery list and put it into an envelope. Then, she would put a split in a piece of long, narrow wood, such as kindling, and the envelope was stuck in the slit. A flag was stuck in the ground some distance from their home which would signal to an approaching train to open the baggage car door. Mrs. Norman would then throw the stick with the envelope into the baggage car. In due course, groceries would arrive and be removed from the baggage car. She must have been a very good aim. Norman further explained that one time, no groceries arrived. It was not discovered until the next spring that the door on the other side of the baggage car had been open so that her envelope had flown right through the car and out the other side, landing in the snow bank. Refrigeration, during summer, was in a nearby ice cave. If they ran out of meat, one of the kids simply went fishing.

Logging was done in the winter, chopped in spring and summer, ready for the following winter.

They did have contact with the outside world because they had a subscription to the Toronto Star, owned a radio, and had a telephone, even though it was a party line. Having a party line wasn't bad because it enabled everyone in section houses along the ACR line to listen in on others' conversations, that way hearing all the local news.

I got the impression that their lives were very happy, without the stress of modern life.

Morley Torgov in his book entitled *A Good Place To Come From*, wrote about being a member of a small group of Jews living in Sault Ste. Marie. His father had been a Russian Jew and found his way to the Sault in 1926 where he established a clothing store on Queen Street East, with the family residing above the store.

The Jewish community lived in the downtown area and owned many of the Sault's best businesses that I remember fondly. Had it not been for those clothing stores, I think most of us would have been ordering through a catalogue. Their businesses are the ones that I remember most from my 1950s childhood in the Sault.

The Jewish people were pillars of our society who gave long hours to our service clubs.

As a child, I knew there was an invisible divide between being of Anglo-Saxon descent and being Italian, or being Protestant and not Catholic. When I started a north end public high school in 1964, we were all mixed together: Indigenous, English, Italian, French, Ukrainian, Finnish, and numerous other types. Religion was never mentioned. It never occurred to us to form ethnic cliques. Perhaps, in particular, it was the sports that dispelled the east vs. west nonsense. There must have been other influences as well such as music classes, the band, as well as various types of school activities such as yearbook and drama.

Torgov described in his book, what I personally did not experience, but did hear about and always

194

thought was bizarre behavior. The following is an excerpt from pages 16 and 17 of Torgov's book which shows the situation far better than I could:

There was little, if any, overt discrimination against the pocket-size Jewish community. Happily for us, the Gentile population was too engrossed in a civil war of its own to pay us much attention. It was a cold war, waged between the
Anglo-Saxons of the East End and the Italians of the West End. The latter group, who numbered many thousands, were beginning to look eastward from the Latin Quarter toward Simpson Street. ... So totally did this conflict occupy the two principal racial establishments that somehow we Jews were able to slip out from between the two sides and maintain a state of neutrality.
On the surface, it was an effortless, uncomplicated existence.
But our fathers and mothers knew otherwise. Fathers and mothers stewed privately and publicly about the love affairs of their sons and daughters: how could young David ever find and settle down with a Jewish girl if, instead of venturing forth to Detroit or Toronto, he stayed put on Queen Street and took out schiksas on Saturday night? What could be done to prevent young Miriam from becoming too involved with that shaygetz from Pim Hill, the fellow with the Irish surname who kept

taking her the Hi-Y dances and Boat Club
regattas? The same people saw each other
all the time. They did the same things all
the time.

As a result, the Jewish children were
encouraged to leave the Sault, attend university
and find a nice Jewish person to marry, and that is
what they did.

I have not determined when the arrival of the
Italians began, but according to Torgov, "hundreds
of immigrants from Italy and Slavic countries" came
to the Sault to work in the steel plant in the 1920s.
Later, post-WW II, many more Italians arrived in
the Sault from southern Italy, where there had
been destruction during the war to the extent that
there were no homes, farms, or businesses so that
the economy had also been completely shattered.
In the Sault, good jobs were to be had, especially at
the steel plant. For obvious reasons, they did not
arrive with heaps of money which was in contrast
to the well-established Anglo-Saxons of the east
end.

Torgov wrote about the problems his family's
maid had because she was Ukrainian and fell in
love with an Italian lad. It was Torgov who
innocently let the cat out of the bag to the girl's
parents. The parents were furious about their
daughter's relationship with an Italian. These west
enders, too, did not accept the Italian people.
Eventually, the couple did marry and continued to
reside in the west end.

At that time in history, the west end was not
considered the place to live. Its people were

immigrants who were poor, struggling to learn a new language, trying to adjust to a harsh winter climate, and culturally very different from other citizens.

F. G. Paci, in his book, *The Italians*, gives an excellent description of what it was like for adults to leave their beautiful southern Italy and resettle in the Sault, or any small Canadian city. Frank Paci grew up in the Sault and has a strong understanding of the Italian culture and struggles in a new country.

I suppose it was fear of the unknown. The established culture knew nothing about the Italian culture and did not care to learn. I really have a problem thinking that those who had money – the east enders – wanted nothing to do with those who did not have money. I am convinced that it was fear of the unknown.

It took some decades, but I would say by the 1960s the problem ended. I believe it was because when all cultures were thrown together in a public high school, those different cultures began to mix and then inter-marry.

The west end actually had a very vibrant society. The kids were heavily into sports, to such an extent that many came to be highly respected and accomplished sportsmen. In particular, Tony and Phil Esposito, with their acclaimed NHL careers, are the examples that come to mind. The Esposito brothers did not learn to play hockey indoors, in an arena on a glassy-surfaced ice. They learned outside, in all types of severe winter weather, in Central Park, which is now named Esposito Park in their honour. I knew that rink because I skated there, given it was within walking distance from my maternal grandmother's home, who being Anglo-Saxon, resided east of Gore Street.

Beyond sports, the Italians became prominent within the city and elsewhere. They became doctors, lawyers, judges, and, dare I forget, restaurateurs that prepared Italian food that cannot be rivalled elsewhere.

The Italians have definitely arrived and the Sault is finer because of them.

The Ferry Is No More

Prior to the construction of the bridge between the two Saults, people crossed the St. Marys River by ferry boat. I remember it well. A vehicle could drive onto the ferry, but from both sides of the river, we often merely walked to the dock, hopped on the ferry, rode over the river, and walked off on the other side right into the downtown shopping district. Once the bridge opened, the culture of the area changed, and in due course, businesses spread up onto the hills on both sides of the river, so that it became necessary to drive. Today, although there is much cross-border activity, the friendly neighbourhood is now rather impersonal. The International Bridge for vehicles opened on October 31, 1962.

Sports

It would take another book to list the Sault's many sports. As a result, I will just list them, but I encourage any sports person or team to seriously look into experiencing sport in the Sault. For teams, in particular, I recommend contacting Sport Tourism Event Management, Tourism Sault Ste. Marie. Whatever the sport, an exceptional event can be created. Here goes the list: snowboarding, skiing: downhill and cross-country, showshoeing, snowmobiling, hockey, curling, ice fishing, fishing, sailing, basketball, baseball, football, soccer, lacrosse, golf, hiking, swimming, biking, ringette, bowling, kayaking, canoeing, white-water river trips, camping. It is possible that I have missed a sport, so just google your sport because my guess is that it's here. For visiting sports folk, we also have the right accommodation for everyone: hotels, motels, campgrounds, bed & breakfast, cottages, and chalets.

The Mountain

Searchmont that is. Superb skiing with a 700-foot vertical, along with all the amenities expected at a first-class ski hill. Check searchmont.com for the whole description. I am sure you will be impressed.

Trail Map provided courtesy of Searchmont Resort.

Culture in the City

If the Sault's economy could rely solely on culture, the city would be extremely wealthy given that the Sault has always had wonderful cultural activities.

Art Gallery of Algoma

This is a superb gallery displaying an array of accomplished visual arts. It has an excellent art collection and its volunteers provide outstanding education and activities. I particularly took note of its Winter Festival of Art 2018, The Gallery invited all artists, whether new or established, to take part in its Light & Shadow exhibition. In arranging this type of exhibition, the staff guide and encourage all artists to create unique opportunities to showcase their artistic talents.

The Gallery showcases about 5,000 artworks including, but not limited to, paintings, sculptures, photographs, and drawings. Displayed works include those of five members of The Group of Seven: Franklin Carmichael, A.J. Casson, A.Y. Jackson, J.E.H. MacDonald, and F. H. Varley. Norval Morrisseau, an Indigenous artist, of Northwestern Ontario, also has a place of pride in the Gallery.

Algoma Fall Festival

Each October, the Algoma Fall Festival presents visual and performing arts, including such acclaimed musicians as Sylvia Tyson and Serena Ryder. Dancing, theatre, visual arts, and education are all part of the Festival. In 2017, Dr. Roberta Bondar's Light in the Land the Nature of Canada was presented. Her landscape photography captures the awe of Canada's natural beauty. Dr.

Bondar, an astronaut from the Sault, flew, in 1992, on board the space shuttle Discovery. In addition to scientific experiments, Dr. Bondar photographed the Earth using various types of cameras. Following her flight in space, she perfected her photographic talent.

Sault Theatre Workshop

The Workshop regularly puts out calls for auditions by the Sault's talent to join locally produced theatrical plays. The cost to attend is minimal and thoroughly enjoyable. Of special interest is the Workshop's annual One Act Festival Workshop which creates the circumstances to learn the skills of acting and directing with professional adjudicating, coaching, and workshops.

Musical Comedy Guild

This is a non-profit entity where people work together to present immensely-polished, professional musical theatrical productions, staring extraordinary local talent. The musically talented actors are a match for other theatre productions anywhere.

Shadows of the Mind

Shadows of the Mind is the Sault's own film festival. This week-long event presents cinema from around the work. It begins on the last Monday of February each year with films being shown at the Grand Theatre, Galaxy Cinemas, and The Tech. The entire list of films, and their viewing locations, is released in early February. The cost to attend is very reasonable and the films are not to be missed by any movie enthusiast.

Sault Symphony Orchestra
This is a joint Canadian-American orchestra of local professional musicians that often performs with internationally recognized soloists. Its programs are performed in venues on both sides of the Sault border. Once per year, in summer, the orchestra presents Beer, Bratwurst & Beethoven which is held outdoors throughout the day and evening.

Northern Arts Academy
Its staff instructs students, privately, or in groups, in singing, piano, acting, and movement, as well as musical theatre training. All instructors are highly accomplished and experts in their respective fields. Classes in voice, acting and movement are offered to three age groups: Primary (age six to eight). Intermediate (ages 9 to 12) and senior (13 to 18).

Musical Groups
The Chamber Singers of Algoma are an especially talented group who have sung at international festivals, as well as at the Vatican, and Carnegie Hall in New York City. The Algoma Festival Choir, The Northland Barbershop Chorus, and The Steeltown Silver Band, are all exceptionally talented and perform concerts throughout the year.

Dance
The popular dance schools are: Studio Dance Arts, Soo Dance Unlimited, Davey Dance Company, and

Elite Dance Force. Studio Dance Arts instructs children of preschool age and upward. Its focus is on dance techniques and performance skills, with both recreational and competitive dance programs. Soo Dance Unlimited offers instruction in ballet, jazz, tap, and hip-hop. Dancers can be anywhere from age 2.5 years to adults. Both recreational and competitive dance is taught. Davey Dance Company accepts children from the age of 2.5 years and introduces them to creative movement and basic ballet. For older children, there is tap, jazz, hip-hop, ballet, and lyrical which combines ballet and jazz. Elite Dance Force teaches children: ballet, pointe, lyrical, contemporary, jazz, tap, and hip-hop, while incorporating social skills, self-esteem, and confidence.

Northern Ontario Country Music Hall of Fame

The Sault has a long history of supporting country music. Fans from northeastern Ontario fill bus size vehicles to attend the annual awards weekend, held at the Quattro Hotel, in the Sault. This is a must-attend for country music fans.

Hub Trail Bridge

By Sheri Minardi Photography

At Fort Creek

John Rowswell Hub Tail Map

Beautiful hiking - biking trail throughout the Sault
Map is from www.hubtrail.com. Check this website
for details of the trail.

Twenty-First Century

In the new millennium, the Sault struggled with existing industry, considered alternative energy, concentrated on attracting new types of industry, and continued to build on tourism. The steel plant continued to fluctuate. The city crept towards the north end which once was fields with a few buildings. Young people left for jobs elsewhere, given a shortage of employment opportunities. Often, obtaining employment in the Sault depends on who you know. Another reason for leaving, as it applied to myself, for example, was that unless a person has a government job or is a member of a union, or a trade, the pay is extremely low. There are very wealthy employers in the private sector who want qualified employees but believe those employees should not earn much above minimum wage because the employer is of the opinion that they are not generating income for the business, which is bizarre thinking considering that, if the owner had to do every aspect of the work himself, he would not have the time to generate a high income.

Movie Making Potential

Various movies have been made in the Sault. I think the most unique result of this is that young local actors gain valuable experience that permits them to obtain credits with the result of membership in ACTRA. The production of local movies also provides those interested in other sectors of movie making the opportunity to observe and participate.

Alternative Energy

Currently, the Sault is billed as the Alternative Energy Capital of North America due to its various types of energy initiatives, being wind, hydroelectric, cogeneration, solar, and reverse polymerization. I look forward to these various renewable energy endeavours to become prominent in the future.

Education

The Sault is the place to be for education due to its endless opportunities.

For those who did not graduate from secondary school, Holy Angels is the answer to their educational woes. This school provides adaptable schedules for all of its students, and every student is provided with whatever amount of instruction and time is required for the student to graduate.

For French speaking children, there is École publique Écho-des-Rapids which is known for its innovative approach to teaching.

French Immersion is offered at certain elementary and secondary schools.

Catholic schools, as well as public schools are available for individual choice.

Sault College has both full and part-time studies. The list of courses available for academics and trades is extensive.

Algoma University is recognized for its diversity and small class sizes. Twenty-seven percent of the student body comes to the Sault from thirty different countries. Shingwauk Kinoomaage Gamig offers courses and programs of particular interest to Indigenous students, in accordance with Chief Shingwauk's efforts, in the 1800s, to secure educational opportunities for his people. The Algoma campus is situated on the grounds of the former Shingwauk Residential School.

The Sault Ste. Marie Economic Development Corporation (SSMEDC)

The SSMEDC was formed to promote the Sault. Its website states, as follows:

Sault Ste. Marie is a great place to do business for a number of reasons. For starters, international consultant KPMG ranked it as one of the top communities in Ontario in an International Competitive Analysis.

For businesses, Sault Ste. Marie offers:

Efficient and diverse transportation systems such as rail, highway, marine and air.

A non-disruptive and efficient border point to the United States via the I-75 and access to the Trans-Canada Highway.

Convenient and direct access to major international airport hubs and international supply chains.

Excellent logistics and manufacturing infrastructure.

Research and operating capacity to access bio-resources.

Direct access to all major fibre optic networks and international fibre optic connections.

Updated zoning bylaws improve local development and allow appropriate zoning to accommodate new businesses and help diversify the local economy.

Government incentives in areas such as technology, innovation, training, site acquisition, infrastructure and manufacturing.

Highly-skilled and technical workforce available, along with modern post-secondary institutions.

Superb quality of life reflecting value and unparalleled opportunities.

The SSMEDC has the expertise to give guidance to those who have a business idea but need help developing it.

Further activity of the SSMEDC is centred on encouraging business and investment from outside the Sault to relocate here.

Tourism is another successful section of the SSMEDC.

* * *

The Future

The Sault is making a strong effort to branch out into various diverse industries. This will take time; however, the people are highly skilled and many are well educated for modern industry. We just need to convince industry to set up shop here.

The website entitled Batchewana.ca, displays the slogan *"Respecting Our Past Ensuring Our Future."* That basically describes their modern purposes. This website explains that historically, the Ojibway women took responsibility for vegetable gardening, meal preparation and attending to their children, while the men hunted and fished, and when necessary, engaged as warriors to protect their families. These Woodlands Ojibway lived in Wigwams, made out of birch bark, as opposed to the belief of many that they lived in Tipis. It was the Great Plains Ojibway who lived in Tipis.

The Algoma Board of Education produced *The Anishinaabe View – In Their Own Words.* Several Ojibway members took part and answered questions put forth by the students of Eastview School, in Sault, Ontario.

Elder Willard Pine, of Garden River, talked about their oral tradition. That is to say, that their history, including beliefs, came down through the many generations from the elders, some of whom were close to 100 years old before dying. His belief is that there are no bad people, only bad choices.

Chief Dean Sayers of the Batchewana First Nation of Ojibway gave an excellent presentation to the students. The Ojibway pronunciation of Bawating was Ba wah ting, with the emphasis on 'ting'. Its meaning was that it was a place where the rapids were and where people gathered in peace to feast, celebrate, visit, and trade items. People gathered at Bawating because it was the centre of the Great Lakes. At that time, travel was by water although locally there were a few trails. Early fall was the busiest meeting time because the white fish were running.

Chief Sayers stated that because Bawating had both coniferous and deciduous trees, the people were experts in creating different types of medicines as both those types of trees provided the means to make medications.

Another thought came to mind when he talked about snowshoes. I doubt that in France, snowshoes were practical. In this area, the Ojibway had already created their type of snowshoes so that the French learned from the Ojibway about this effective method of dealing with deep snow when the lakes and rivers were impassable to canoes.

The Robinson Huron Treaty of 1850 never worked out well for the Indigenous. I know of cases where the government sold land to Non-Indigenous people that had been reserved for the Indigenous people.

Many cases of this happened.

In 1867 Canada became a country and hired men to be 'Indian Agents' who were to police the Indians for Canada. Part of their job was to assimilate the 'Indians' by turning them into 'whites'. The Indigenous live on Reserves but cannot own the land. Canada owns it. To be clear, certain tracts of land were reserved for the benefit of the Indians but owned by Canada.

No other group of people in this country would ever tolerate that mentality.

In 2014, pursuant to the terms of the Robinson Huron Treaty, the Indigenous sued Canada, as well as Ontario, for their fair share of revenue, retroactively, stemming from Indigenous resources controlled by Canada. In 1850, there was about $20,000 for Canada to invest, at 6% per year. The interest generated from this was to be added to the existing annual payment to be paid to the Indigenous.

During the 1840s, mining companies conducted their activity along the shores of lakes Superior and Huron. The governments did nothing to stop it. The Indigenous took this matter into their own hands and travelled to Mica Bay, on Lake Superior, to halt the mining work. The government responded by establishing a Commission to document the Indigenous peoples' claims but also to find a way for the government to pursue advantages for itself. Thomas Anderson was the Indian Superintendent at the time. He stated that the government wanted to "extinguish the Indian right, by a treaty granting the Aboriginals an equitable remuneration for the whole country."

There was an "escalator clause" in the Robinson Huron Treaty that specified that if the lands "at any future period produce such an amount as will enable the Government of the Province, without incurring loss, to increase the annuity hereby secured to them, then and in that case the same shall be augmented from time to time."

This did not happen.

In 1851, Chief Shingwauk inquired of the government as to why the extra amount of annuity had not been paid when new mines were opened. The same question was put to the government by others ever since.

Again, nothing happened.

There is a limit to individual payments but not to the band (or Indian Nation) as a whole.

Therein lies the problem.

There was never an accounting by the government as to the interest earned on the original annuity principal amount and never an indication that the government could not increase the principal annuity amount by applying the "escalator clause."

The amount of revenue that Ontario and Canada earned from the lands since 1850 has to be calculated.

Although the Indigenous requested that the Trial be paused while the monetary amount could be negotiated, Canada rejected this proposal.

I can only assume that Canada hopes to pay nothing. So, on went the trial.

A court judgment is expected in December, 2018.

About the Author

Sandra Rousseau combined her skills of researching, interviewing, writing, and editing to create a career as an author, after working for 35 years in law, both in Canada and the U.S.

Her extensive research extending back into the 8th century follows a family of Vikings attacking Normandy, followed by England in 1066 with William the Conqueror, and in the 12th century relocating to Scotland, then to Northern Ireland in the 17th century, followed by North America in the mid-19th century, resulted in a millennium of history.

The bloodless offence against Mackinac Island during the War of 1812 – 1814, of which her paternal ancestors took part, inspired her to conduct detailed research into the daily reports written by officers involved in the war, and write the historical book entitled *American Attempt to Take Canada,* which became a best-seller between spring and fall of 2012.

Children of the Fallen Snow was her next research project which delved into her French and Indigenous paternal ancestry. Research discovered her ancestral familial connection with Tecumseh, as well as Ottawa Chief Me-sa-sa, both of whom fought against the settlers' expansion in Ohio. The Battle of Fallen Timbers, on August 20, 1794, is considered to have been the last battle of the

American Revolution. Me-sa-sa's life ended, as he stood on what became known as Turkey Foot Rock, while rallying his warriors, when General Anthony Wayne's army shot him off the rock. Tecumseh went on to fight in Canada in the War of 1812 – 1814 and was ultimately killed in the Battle of the Thames River. Then, through in-depth research and testing of various people, Sandra uncovered her Indigenous DNA, which goes back thousands of years in North America.

Book Sales at Superior Sensations Café

Westport Café soon to be Superior Sensations Café
Station Mall, Bay Street, Sault Ste. Marie, Ontario

Adrian Huffels (left) owner of Superior Sensations
Café, with Corey Marques, Publisher of Awaken Ink
Inc.

You may purchase books published by
Awaken Ink Inc. at Superior Sensations Café and, at
the same time, enjoy a delicious cup of their
numerous varieties of coffee or tea, along with
other specialties on the menu.

Below is Leah Johnson, co-owner of Superior Sensations Café, taking a break, during preparation of their menu.

If you found this book enjoyable, interesting, and informative, you might want to read my book entitled *American Attempt to Take Canada, War of 1812 – 1814, St. Joseph Island, Mackinac Island, Sault Ste. Marie.*

The War of 1812 – 1814 as it happened on upper Lake Huron. The start of the war was a bloodless offence against Mackinac Island. Then, the pressure was on the Canadians to defend this island, their interests in the vicinity, and the borders of Canada.

Reviews of *American Attempt to Take Canada, War of 1812 – 1814*

Sandra Rousseau's *American Attempt to Take Canada, War of 1812 – 1814* is a lively and fascinating history of a neglected part of the War of 1812, namely the struggle between Canada and the U.S. in the upper Lake Huron region. The author presents detailed accounts of military actions in the region as well as background on the soldiers, sailors, fur traders, and Native participants. I highly recommend this book for those interested in Canadian and upper Great Lakes history and biography.
- Dr. W. Stephen McBride, Camp Nelson Civil War Heritage Park and McBride Preservations Services

"I encountered Sandra Rousseau several years ago while researching for a novel set in the time of the famous 1812 attack on Fort Michilimackinac. Her apparent grasp of the subject was so complete, I was compelled to contact her directly and profited greatly from the ensuing association. Ms. Rousseau has now expanded on her research in an easy to read monograph that puts to rest any doubt about the intentions of the Americans or the resolve of the Canadians before and during that conflict.

The background leading to the war is set out in clarity. I liked the way she breathes life into the major players, particularly Robert Dickson, John Askew, Captain Charles Roberts. Her treatment of these and others populating the fur trade routes, make the reading of history come alive.

Rousseau tends to examine events from more than one aspect, there being those of the Americans, the English Canadians, the French, and the Natives. She explains the importance of the fur trade to all sides, particularly the Americans who needed the fort on Mackinac Island to assure trade route superiority. Her treatment of the preparations for and the actual attack by the Canadians and Ojibwa from St. Joseph Island is not the first to be written but is told in clear context. I don't believe an interested reader will find a more thorough or personal rendering of this subject.

For anyone interested in the war if 1812, I highly recommend Sandra Rousseau's well-written treatment."

-Richard Whitten Barnes, Author of Mysteries and Historical Fiction. New for 2018 MEDALLION

"In Canada, much of the attention of the bicentenary of the War of 1812 is limited to a few regions, most notably, the Niagara Peninsula. It is often forgotten that the North West encompassed

a vast area that witnessed a number of important actions; the <u>American Attempt to Take Canada</u> examines, in general terms, the wartime events at St. Joseph Island, Mackinac Island, Sault Ste. Marie and naval events in Georgian Bay. By no means a scholarly study, this . . . is a fine example of local history, and provides a good introduction to the war in (the) area around Sault Ste. Marie."
Review of Sandra Rousseau's first edition book entitled *American Attempt to Take Canada: War of 1812 – 1814*, as reviewed in the War of 1812 Magazine, Issue 19, December, 2012.
-Major John R. Grodzinski, CD, BA, Ma, Ph. D, **Assistant Professor, Department of History, Royal Military College of Canada.**

Bibliography

Abbott, John, Mount, Graeme S., Mulloy, Michael J., *The Border at Sault Ste. Marie*. Toronto, Dundurn Press, 1995.

Abbott, John, Mount, Graeme S., Mulloy, Michael J., *The History of Fort St. Joseph*. Toronto, Dundurn Press, 2000.

Algoma Board of Education. *The Anishinaabe View – In Their Own Words*. Produced by the Board and presented on youtube.com.

Arbic, Bernie; City of the Rapids: Sault Ste. Marie's Heritage. Allegan Forest, MI: The Priscilla Press, 2003.

Askin, John (1739 – 1815) *The John Askin Papers Vol. 2*. Burton Historical Records. Quaife, Milo Milton, Editor. Detroit. Published by Detroit Library Commission 1928 - 1931.

Bayliss, Joseph, Bayliss, Estelle, *Historic St. Joseph Island*. Cedar Rapids, Iowa. Torch Press, 1938.

Bayliss, Joseph, Bayliss, Estelle, Quaif, Milo; *River of Destiny*. Detroit: Wayne State University Press, 1955.

Batchewana.ca website of the Batchewana First Nation of Ojibways.

Beth Jacob Synagogue – see Congregation.

Bethune, Brian (November 21, 2011). Review: The Codex Canadensis and the Writings of Louis Nicolas. Book by François-Marc Gagnon with Nancy Senior and Réal Ouellet. *Macleans Magazine.*

Butterfield, C.W. *Brûlé's Discoveries and Explorations 1610–1626.* Helman-Taylor, 1898.

Chute, Janet E.; *The Legacy of Shingwaukonse, A Century of Native Leadership.* University of Toronto Press Incorporated 1998.

Champlain Society, The; *The Journal of Gabriel Franchère.* Toronto. 1969.

Channing and Lansing; *The Story of the Great Lakes,* p. 331. (re: official report coureur do bois in 1680).

City of Sault Ste. Marie, Ontario, website, being www.cityssm.on.ca/library.

Congregation Beth Jacob, Unaffiliated. www.bethjacobssm.ca.Conway, Thor. *Spirits on Stone, Lake Superior Ojibway History, Legends and the Agawa Pictographs.* San Luis Obispo, California. Heritage Discoveries Publications, 2010.

Cruikshank, Lieut.-Col. E. (1853 – 1939). *An Episode of the War of 1812. The Story of the Schooner "Nancy"* Publisher: Ontario Historical Society.

Canadian Archives, Series C, Volume 685, pages 138, 145 and 168: letter from Lt.-Gen. Drummond to Noah Freer; Letter from George Crookshank to Peter Turquand, Deputy Commissary General; letter from Lt.-Col. Drummond to Sir George Prevost.
Canadian Archives, Series M. Volume 6, page 202 as to Lieutenant Worsley's reporting letter to Sir James L. Yeo. Series C, Volume 685, page 172.

Dawson. K.C.A.: see Parks Canada.

Dalla Bona, Luke. *Stage I & II Archaeological Assessment of the Gros Cap Bluffs Property, Prince Township, Ontario*. November 7, 2001.

Fowle, Otto; *Sault Ste. Marie and Its Great Waterway*. New York: G.P. Putnam's Sons, 1925.

Franchère, Gabriel, (1786 – 1863). *Journal of a voyage on the northwest coast of North America during the years 1811, 1812, 1813, 1814*. Publications of the Champagne Society, 45. Editor: Lamb, William Kaye. Toronto, 1969.

Heath, Frances M.; *Sault Ste. Marie City By The Rapids*. Burlington, ON: Windsor Publications (Canada) Ltd. 1988.

Henry, Alexander; *Travels and Adventures in Canada And The Indian Territories Between The Years 1760 and 1776.* Edmonton. M.G. Hurtig Ltd., Booksellers & Publishers.

Henry, Alexander: *Travels and Adventures in the Years 1760-1776.* Ed. M.M. Quaife; Chicago: R.R. Donnelly, 1921

Jameson, Mrs. (Anna) 1794-1860: *Winter studies and summer rambles in Canada.* Toronto: Coles Publishing Co. 1972.

Iles, Elizabeth A.: *Ask the Grey Sisters Sault Ste. Marie and the General Hospital 1898 – 1998.*Dundurn Press, Toronto, 1998.

Jesuits: The Jesuit Relations and Allied Document; travels and explorations of the Jesuit missionaries in North America, 1610-1791. New York: Vanguard Press, 1954.

John Askin Papers 1796 - 1820, Vol. II. Editor: Quaife, Milo M. Burton Historical Records. Detroit. Published by Library Commission 1931.
Lane, Peter: see Parks Canada.

J.S. McGivern, "BARAGA, FREDERIC," in *Dictionary of Canadian Biography*, vol. 9, University of Toronto/Université Laval, 2003–, accessed January 15, 2018,
www.biographi.ca/en/bio/baraga_frederic_9E.html

Michigan Pioneer and Historical Collection, vol. xiv, p. 644 – letter of the Minister of Foreign Affairs at Paris, to the Marquis Du Quesne, then Governor General of Canada. The letter is dated June 16, 1752. The editor of Alexander Henry's book stated: "A curious story about one of Cadotte's grandchildren is told in Kingston's Western Wanderings, vol. 1, p. 235.

Minnesota Historical Collections, vol. v, p. 434. (re: French fort at the Sault 1750).

Newman, Peter C.: *Caesars of the wilderness*. New York: Penguin Books, 1987.

Norman, Norma C.: *The Canyon Years 1925 – 1941 A Collection of Children's Memories of Life in the Agawa Canyon*. H.G. McNeek Publishing, Wyoming, Ontario, 2003.

Ontario Archives, George Gordon papers, MU 1146G, Moffat, Fort William, to George Gordon, Montontagué, 25 July 1809.

Osborne, A. C., *The Migration of Voyageurs from Drummond Island to Penetanguishene in 1828*. Originally published by the Ontario Historical Society Papers and Records Volume III Published by the Society in Toronto in 1901, Pages 123 – 166.

Parks Canada Manuscript Report Number 439, entitled Pukaskwa National Park and the Prehistory of the North Shore of Lake Superior by K.C.A. Dawson, 1979, and Archaeological Survey in Proposed Development Areas, Pukaskwa National Park by Peter Lane and Harley Stark, 1977. Also see Wright, James V.

Parks Canada Agency, G. Vandervlugt, H.06.644.09.01(08), 2001. Research Report Number 1981-SUB. Historic Sites and Monuments Act (R.S.C., 1985, c. H-4). Designation Date: 1981-11-13. People: Ojibway. Whitefish Island (Designation Name). Whitefish Island National Historic Site of Canada.

Richard E. Ruggle, "McMURRAY, WILLIAM," in *Dictionary of Canadian Biography*, vol. 12, University of Toronto/Université Laval, 2003–, accessed January 15, 2018, www.biographi.ca/en/bio/mcmurray_william_12E.html.

Silcox, David P.: *The Group of Seven and Tom Thomson*, Firefly Books, 2003.

Stark, Harley: see Parks Canada.

Stewart, W. Brian: *The Ermatingers A 19th-Century Ojibway-Canadian Family*. UBC Press, The University of British Columbia, Vancouver, B.C., 2007.

Torgov, Morley: *A Good Place to Come From*. Lester and Orpen Limited, Toronto, 1974.

Van Kirk, Sylvia: *Many Tender Ties Women in Fur-Trade Society, 1670 – 1870*. Watson & Dwyer Publishing Ltd. Winnipeg, Manitoba. 1980.

Warren, William W., 1825–1853, *History of the Ojibway People*. Minnesota Historical Society Press, St. Paul, MN. 1984. Borealis Books.

Winsor, Justin, 1831-1897, Harvard University Librarian: The pageant of Saint Lusson, Sault Ste. Marie, 1671: an address delivered at the annual commencement of the University of Michigan, June 30, 1892. Ann Arbor, MI: Board of regents, 1892.

Wright, James V. 1972. The Shield Archaic. National Museum of Canada Publications in Archaeology, No. 3, Ottawa. The author attempts to demonstrate the existence and nature of an Archaic tradition called the Shield Archaic. The tradition occupied one-third of Canada for most of its Prehistory and was directly responsible for later, non-archaic developments.

Wright, James V. 1972. Ontario Prehistory, An Eleven Thousand Year Archaeological Outline. National Museum of Canada, Ottawa. Written for the general public, Ontario Prehistory provides a descriptive outline of Prehistoric life in Ontario preceding the time of European contact. The author describes the people and events of the Palaeo, Archaic, Initial Woodland and Terminal Woodland periods in both Northern and Southern Ontario. He demonstrates the different ecological adaptations assumed by the inhabitants of the two regions. The book is well illustrated with pictures, maps and charts.

Index

Made in the USA
Monee, IL
12 June 2021